Helen Hadkins and Samantha Lewis

Interactive

Student's Book 1

CAMBRIDGE
UNIVERSITY PRESS

Contents

Quick Start

1

🔊 **1.1** Look at pictures 1–3. Complete the sentences with the verb *be*. Then listen and check.

1 Hello! My name .... Laura and I .... thirteen. These .... my two cats. They .... very friendly.

2 This .... my room. It .... quite small and there .... lots of books and posters on the walls.

3 Those .... my brothers. Andy .... ten and David .... fifteen. We .... British, but my mum .... from Colombia.

2

a Complete the sentences. Use *There's* or *There are* and the singular or plural form of the nouns.

table   sandwich   boy   book   poster   child

1 .... a .... on Laura's bed.

2 .... a lot of .... on the wall.

3 .... three .... in Laura's family.

4 .... two .... in the garden.

5 .... a blue .... in the garden.

6 .... some .... on the table.

b Work with a partner. Guess what is in your partner's bag today.

> *I think there are three books in your bag.*   > *Yes, that's right.*   > *No, there's one book.*

3

a Put the words in order and write the questions.

1 a / is / teenager / Laura ?

....

2 are / Laura's / cats / friendly ?

....

3 tall / Andy / is ?

....

4 black / jeans / are / David's ?

....

5 garden / in / parents / the / Laura's / are ?

....

6 Laura's / Britain / is / from / mother ?

....

b Write two more *Is/Are* questions about pictures 1–3.

c Work with a partner. Ask and answer the questions in Exercises 3a and 3b.

> *Is Laura a teenager?*   > *Yes, she is.*

4

Complete the sentences with possessive adjectives.

Andy: I've got blue jeans and .... T-shirt is red. ①

David: We live in South London. .... house is in Ross Street. ②

Laura: I've got two cats. .... names are Lulu and Baz. ③

Mum: David and Andy! .... sandwiches are on the table. ④

Dad: That's Laura. Andy and David are .... brothers. ⑤

5

a 🔊 1.2 Listen to David. Are the sentences right (✓) or wrong (✗)?

1 He's Laura's sister. ☐
2 He can play football. ☐
3 He's got lots of magazines. ☐

4 She can't speak Spanish. ☐
5 She can play the piano. ☐

6 He can sing. ☐
7 He hasn't got a guitar. ☐
8 He's got football posters in his room. ☐

b Make five true sentences from the table.

I		blonde hair
My English teacher	can	brown eyes
My parents	has got	swim
(name of friend)	have got	a dog and a cat
(friend) and (friend)	hasn't got	a good computer
My aunt and uncle	haven't got	play the guitar
(famous person)		a red car

6

Write pronouns for the <u>underlined</u> words.

1 Please close <u>the window</u>.　　Please close ....
2 Look at <u>my brother</u>.　　Look at ....
3 <u>The books</u> are on my desk.　　............... 're on my desk
4 Come with <u>Mike and me</u>.　　Come with ....
5 <u>My uncle</u> is Italian.　　............... 's Italian.
6 <u>Jane and I</u> love <u>chocolate</u>.　　............... love ....
7 <u>My mother</u> likes <u>cats</u>.　　............... likes ....

7

🔊 1.3 Read the conversations and circle the correct word(s). Then listen and check.

Laura: Where ¹............ my folders? I can't see ²............ .
Mum: ³............ on the table in ⁴............ room.

1 **A** is 　**B** are 　**C** can
2 **A** this 　**B** him 　**C** them
3 **A** They're 　**B** Their 　**C** There are
4 **A** Andy 　**B** Andy's 　**C** Andys

David: Is ⁵............ Eva's brother?
Andy: Yes. His name ⁶............ Sebastian.
David: I like ⁷............ T-shirt. It's cool!

5 **A** that 　**B** there 　**C** the
6 **A** is 　**B** it's 　**C** has got
7 **A** its 　**B** his 　**C** him

Man: ⁸............ help you?
Dad: ⁹............ a hamburger, please.
Man: Right. ¹⁰............ you like a drink?
Dad: No, thanks.

8 **A** I can 　**B** Can I 　**C** Am I
9 **A** I've got 　**B** I'm 　**C** I'd like
10 **A** Have 　**B** Are 　**C** Would

Grammar reference:
Workbook pages 78, 80, 96

Me and my family

Present simple: *I/you/we/they*
Present simple: questions
Vocabulary: Family; Everyday things
Interaction 1: Asking for personal information

1 Read and listen

The Qu family

The Torres family

a Read the four texts about the families quickly and match them with the pictures.

1 My name's Nadira and I'm 15. I live with my parents, Frances and Mustapha, and my two sisters, Iman and Miriam. Miriam is 17 and Iman is 10. We live in a house in Cambridge, England. My parents both work and I study and go out with my friends at weekends. ☐

2 I live with my wife, Pauline, in Kenya. My name's Boniface. We've got two daughters, Joyce and Sharon. Joyce is eight and Sharon is 16 months old. I work in Nairobi and I drive a taxi from 4:30am until 10pm. I love my job. ☐

b 🔊 **1.4** Read the texts again and listen. Complete the information about the families.

The Amrani family
Number of people _____
Ages of children _____
Country _____
Pets **✗** _____

The Qu family
Number of people _____
Ages of children _____
Country _____
Pets _____

The Kamau family
Number of people _____
Ages of children _____
Country _____
Pets **✗** _____

The Torres family
Number of people _____
Ages of children _____
Country _____
Pets _____

Culture Vulture

Did you know that in some countries (the UK and Australia) people have one surname, but in other countries (Spain and Peru) people have two? In some countries (China and Japan) the surname comes first. How many surnames have you got?

The Amrani family

The Kamau family

3 I'm 17 and my name is Chen. I live with my mother, Guifang, my father, Wansheng, and my grandfather, Huanjun. We live in an old house in Beijing, China. I haven't got any brothers or sisters but I've got a dog called Guaiguai. I like Saturdays because my uncles and aunts come and we cook a big dinner. ☐

4 My name's Angelo and I'm 16. I've got a little sister called Veronica. She's three. We live with our mother, Raiza, and our two cats in a big flat in Caracas, Venezuela. My grandfather, Ricardo, and my grandmother, Marisol, live with us. I don't like football, but I like planes and cars and I want to be a pilot. ☐

2 Vocabulary

Family

a 🔊 1.5 Look at the texts in Exercise 1a and complete the table. Then listen and check.

Women/Girls	Men/Boys
mother	
	husband
	grandfather
granddaughter	grandson
sister	
	son
aunt	
cousin	cousin

b Correct the sentences.

1 Iman is Nadira's brother.

....

2 Guifang is Chen's grandmother.

....

3 Marisol is Angelo's aunt.

....

4 Sharon is Joyce's mother.

....

5 Frances and Mustapha are Veronica's parents.

....

Check it out!

Possessive 's

The position of the apostrophe (') changes in the plural.

● singular: *Sharon's sister. The girl's father.*
● plural: *The boys' mother.*

c Write five true sentences about the families in Exercise 1a.

⤑ *Huanjun is Wansheng's father.*

d Work with a partner. Read your sentences but don't say the last word. Can your partner say the word?

A: *Veronica is Angelo's …*   B: *Sister.*

3 Speak

a Draw your family tree.

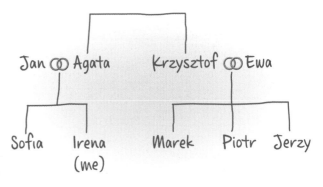

b Work with a partner. Ask and answer questions about your family trees.

A: *Who's Piotr?*   B: *He's my cousin.*

(4) Grammar

Present simple: I/you/we/they

a Look at the examples and complete the table.

> ....⟩ I **go** out with my friends at weekends.
> We **live** in Beijing.
> I **don't like** football.

Positive

I	
You	....
We	....
They	**like**

Negative

I		**go**
You		**live**
We	.... (do not)	**like**
They		

(Circle) the correct word to complete the rule.

- We use the present simple for **permanent** / **temporary** situations, regular or repeated actions, and facts.

b Complete the sentences with the verbs in the present simple.

> not go   live   play   not speak
> not walk   watch   write

1 They .... in London, England.
2 I .... an email to my cousin every week.
3 I .... to school at weekends.
4 They .... to school, they go by bus.
5 I .... TV in the evening.
6 We .... football at my school.
7 They .... French or German.

c Write true sentences about you. Use the verbs in the box.

> go   like   live   play   speak   watch

> ....⟩ I play football.

(5) Vocabulary

Everyday things

a 🔊 1.6 Match the words with the pictures. Then listen and check.

> 1 bicycle 2 camera 3 clock 4 keys 5 lamp 6 mobile
> 7 newspaper 8 photo 9 television 10 umbrella

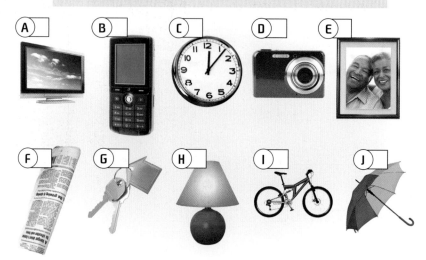

b Do you know any more words for everyday things? Write them down.

c Write sentences about the picture. Use the words in the box and read the Check it out! box.

> clock   keys   lamp   magazines   mobile   newspaper
> photo   television

> ....⟩ There's a lamp in the picture, but there isn't a newspaper.

Check it out!

There is / There are
With *there* use the correct form of the verb *be*.
- singular: **There's** *a lamp.* **There isn't** *a lamp.*
- plural: **There are** *some keys.* **There aren't** *any keys.*

6 Listen

a 🔊 **1.7** Look at the picture. Listen to the quiz show. Can you guess the person's name?

b 🔊 **1.7** Listen again and complete the sentences.

I live with my .... , uncle and ....
I've ....
a .... owl and
....
.... friends.

7 Grammar

Present simple: questions

a Look at the examples and complete the table.

⤑ A: **Do** you **live** in a house?   B: Yes, I **do**.   A: Where **do** you **live**?   B: I **live** in England.

Yes/No questions		**Short answers**
.... I/you/we/they	**live** in Italy? **play** football?	Yes, I/you/we/they .... No, I/you/we/they **don't (do not)**.

Information questions	**Answers**
Where .... I/you/we/they .... ?	I/You/We/They **live** in Poland.

Circle the correct words to complete the rules.

- For *Yes/No* questions and information questions **always/never** use *do*.
- For **Yes/No questions / information questions** always use a question word: *who, what, where, why* and *how*.

Grammar reference: Workbook page 84

b Put the words in the correct order.

1 go / Do / the cinema / you / to ?

....

2 like / Do / you / computers ?

....

3 play / football / Do / you ?

....

4 magazines / Do / read / you ?

....

5 listen / Do / to / you / the radio ?

....

6 go / Do / on / school / you / Saturday / to ?

....

c Write true answers for the questions in Exercise 7b.

d 🔊 **1.8** Match the two parts of the questions. Then listen and check.

1 When	A do you live?
2 What	B do you live with?
3 Who	C CDs do you have?
4 Where	D do you start school?
5 How many	E do you do at the weekend?

e Write true answers for the questions in Exercise 7d.

(8) Pronunciation 🔘DVD

The schwa /ə/ at the end of words

a 🔊 **1.9** Listen to the /ə/ sound at the end of these words.

moth**er** pic**ture** Keny**a**
/ə/   /ə/   /ə/

b 🔊 **1.10** Listen and (circle) the words with the /ə/ sound at the end.

father sister China country brother photo camera taxi daughter dinner

c 🔊 **1.11** Listen and check. Listen and repeat.

d 🔊 **1.12** Listen and repeat.   *She's got a sister in China and a brother in Kenya.*

Interaction 1 🔘DVD

Asking for personal information

a 🔊 **1.13** Listen to the interview and choose the correct answer: A or B.

1 Ⓐ  Ⓑ

6 Ⓐ  Ⓑ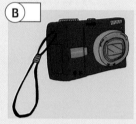

2 Ⓐ 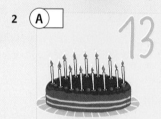 Ⓑ

7 Ⓐ  Ⓑ

3 Ⓐ  Ⓑ

b 🔊 **1.14** Put the words in the correct order. Then listen and check.

1 your / What's / name ?

....

2 are / How / you / old ?

....

3 live / do / Where / you ?

....

4 with / live / Who / you / do ?

....

5 pet / you / Have / got / a ?

....

4 Ⓐ  Ⓑ

6 your / thing / favourite / What's ?

....

7 languages / speak / What / you / do ?

....

5 Ⓐ  Ⓑ

c Work with a partner.
Student A: Turn to page 120. Student B: Turn to page 122.

Portfolio 1

A note for a message board

a Kasia, Luiz, Fiorenza and Dimitri are in England. Read the chat page and match the sentences with the messages.

A 'I understand English.'   **C** 'The food isn't good.'

B 'I like the food.'   **D** 'I like my host family.'

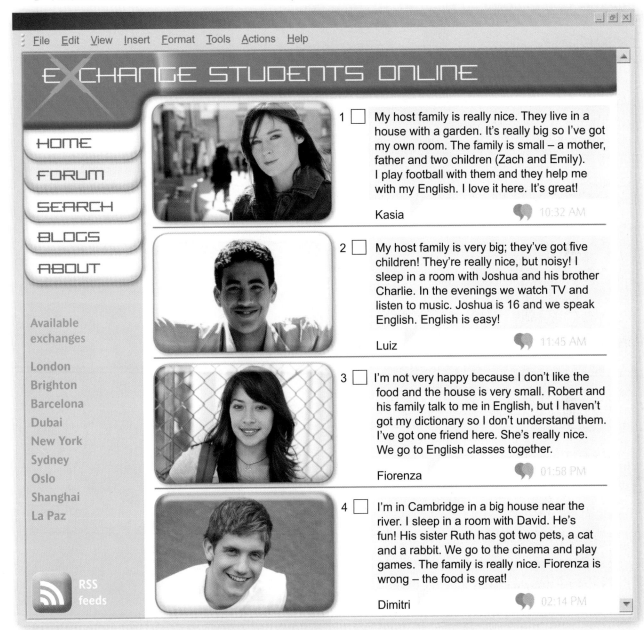

b Look at the examples. Then complete the sentences.

> I sleep in a room with Joshua **and** his brother Charlie.
> I'm not very happy **because** I don't like the food.
> They're really nice, **but** noisy!
> It's really big **so** I've got my own room.

1 I like Spanish music, ... I don't speak Spanish.

2 I've got a TV .... a computer in my room.

3 I haven't got a CD player .... I can't listen to music.

4 I like the family .... they are nice.

c Imagine you are with a host family in the UK. Write a note (35–50 words) for a message board. Use the messages in Exercise a and the words in Exercise b to help you. Write about:

- your host family
- the things you do
- the things you like
- the things you don't like

Drayton Manor THEME PARK
www.draytonmanor.co.uk

Drayton Manor The...

RIDES & ATTRACTIONS

ROLLERCOASTERS
Shockwave • G-Force

WATER RIDES
Splash Canyon • Stormforce 10

SCENIC RIDES
Pirate Adventure • The Haunting
Excalibur • Shoot Out

THRILL RIDES
Maelstrom • Apocalypse

OPENING TIMES

Drayton Manor Theme Park

is open from 15th March to 2nd November.

Gates open at 9.30am
Rides open from 10.30am–5 or 6.00pm.

Please note that the theme park is CLOSED on the 15th, 16th, 22nd, 23rd, 29th, 30th September and 6th, 7th, 13th, 14th, 20th and 21st October (the zoo will be open).

March

Mon	-	3	10	17	24	31
Tues	-	4	11	18	25	-
Wed	-	5	12	19	26	-
Thurs	-	6	13	20	27	-
Fri	-	7	14	21	28	-
Sat	1	8	15	22	29	-
Sun	2	9	16	23	30	-

☐ Open   ■ Closed

ENTRY TICKETS

Adult (age 12+)	£25.00
Child (age 4-11)	£21.00
Grandee (age 60+)	£12.00
Disabled Visitor & Helper (each)	£19.00
Under 4	FREE

Drayton Manor Zoo

With over a hundred species of animal from all over the world, Drayton Manor Zoo is a fascinating place to visit. Come and see:

Exotic creature reserve

Monkeys
  Reptiles
BIG cats
  Eagles
Owls **Parrots**

You can also visit the Discovery Centre where you will come face to face with the wonders of nature and conservation.

HEIGHT RESTRICTIONS

Apocalypse (stand up)	1.4 metres
(sit down)	1.2 metres
Maelstrom	1.3 metres
Shockwave	1.4 metres
G-Force	1.3 metres

where to eat

With many different places to satisfy your appetite, with healthy eating & fresh food menus, we can provide you with the choices to suit you & your family.

PEEL PLAZA

THE CAFETERIA

All day breakfasts, fish & chips, roasts, daily freshly cooked specials, children's meals, large salad & fruit counter, sandwiches, a large selection of snacks, Pepsi drinks, juices, Café Bar coffee. Air conditioned with seating for 200 & patio for 60. Toilets & M&B room.
Vegetarian options available each day.

AERIAL PARK

CEDAR FISH AND CHIP RESTAURANT

Fresh, traditionally cooked fish & chips, pies, kebabs, Pepsi drinks, Café Bar coffee & tea. Seating for 150 inside & 100 seater outdoor patio. Toilets all include mother and baby room.

CENTRAL PLAZA

RAINFOREST PIZZERIA

Pizzas, chicken pieces, baked potatoes, childrens specials, potato wedges. Pepsi, cold drinks, various bottled drinks, tea & coffee, fruit selection. A themed food court with animated action set within 180 seat forest and outside patio (picnic tables). Toilets & M&B room.
Vegetarian options available each day.

ACTION PARK

MINER'S CHICKEN DINER AND TAKEAWAY

Chicken pieces, curly fries & children's specials. Pepsi drinks, Café Bar coffee and tea. Sweets & snacks. Ice Blast. Toilets, patio seating and picnic tables nearby. Vegetarian options available each day.

■ Open daily   ■ Open weekends and holidays

1 Culture UK: Drayton Manor

a Look at the noticeboard about Drayton Manor Theme Park and Drayton Manor Zoo and answer the questions.

1 Can you visit Drayton Manor on October 14th?
2 What animals can you see at the zoo?
3 How many water rides are there?
4 How much is a ticket for a 16-year-old?
5 What food can you eat in Aerial Park?
6 How many days is the park open in March?
7 John is 1.25 metres tall. Which ride can he go on?
8 How many hours are the rides open every day?

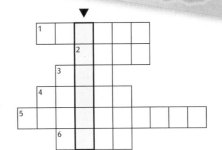

Drayton
Manor

b Complete the puzzle and find the mystery word.

1 You can see these at the zoo.
2 Tickets for children under four are ....
3 Drayton Manor is a park and ....
4 Drayton Manor is open from .... to November.
5 You can stand up on the .... ride.
6 The Cafeteria is in the .... Plaza.

c Work with a partner. Imagine you are at Drayton Manor together. Answer the questions.

1 Which four things do you want to do?
2 Where do you want to eat?
3 How much are your tickets?

2 Your project

A theme park

a Work in a group. Find information about a theme park in your country.

Look for this information:
- the opening times
- a map of the park
- the rides and attractions
- the prices
- where you can eat
- other information

b Make a poster about a theme park in your country. Include the information from Exercise 2a.

2 A day in my life

Present simple: *he/she/it*
Adverbs of frequency
Vocabulary: Daily activities; School subjects
Interaction 2: Asking about routines

1 Vocabulary

Daily activities

a 🔊 **1.15** Match the words with the pictures. Then listen and check.

1 do homework
2 get dressed
3 get up
4 go online
5 go out with friends
6 go to bed
7 go to school
8 have breakfast
9 have a shower
10 listen to music

b Put the activities in order for your day.

c Do you know any more daily activities? Write them down.

d Work with a partner. Ask and answer the questions.

1 Which activities do you do on school days?
2 Which activities do you do at the weekend?

Culture Vulture

Did you know that some British children and teenagers go online for more than five hours a day? How many hours a day do you use the internet?

2 Speak

Work with a partner. Ask and answer questions about the activities in Exercise 1a.

A: *What time do you get up?*
B: *At half past seven.*

Check it out!

Telling the time

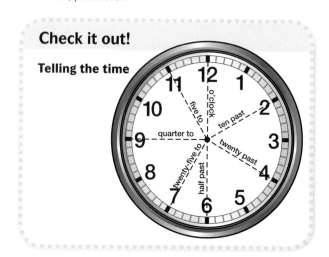

③ Read and listen

a Read the text 'Circus girl' quickly and match a title with each paragraph. There is one extra title.

- **A** No school!
- **B** Mei Li's morning
- **C** Mei Li, the acrobat
- **D** Mei Li's family
- **E** After work

b 🔊 **1.16** Read the text again and listen. Are the sentences about Mei Li *right* (✓), *wrong* (✗) or *doesn't say* (–)?

1 She lives in China. ☐
2 She can walk on her hands. ☐
3 She goes to bed at 11pm. ☐
4 She sees her friends at weekends. ☐
5 She doesn't speak to her family often. ☐
6 She likes the people in the circus. ☐

CIRCUS GIRL

1 ....

Zhang Mei Li is 16 years old and she comes from China. She is an acrobat in a Chinese circus and she can walk and stand on her hands. Mei Li is very strong; she can stand on one hand for seven minutes.

2 ....

Mei Li lives with the other acrobats. She finishes work at 10pm. After work she has a shower and has dinner. Then she sometimes watches a DVD or plays computer games with her friends. She goes to bed very late, usually after midnight.

3 ....

Mei Li doesn't go to school but she has a special teacher. He travels with the circus and teaches all the children in the morning. Mei Li likes English and Chinese, but she thinks Maths is difficult so she studies it a lot. She does her homework in the afternoon, after her classes. At weekends she goes out with her friends to the cinema or to a café.

4 ....

Mei Li doesn't live with her family. Her parents and sister live in Shanghai so she doesn't see them very often. 'But I speak to them on the phone and we write lots of emails,' she says. Mei Li misses her family in Shanghai but she loves the circus. 'I love my family but everyone in the circus is really nice,' she says.

④ Grammar

Present simple: *he/she/it*

a Look at the examples and complete the table.

> *Mei Li **lives** with the other acrobats.*
> *After dinner Mei Li **watches** a DVD.*
> *Mei Li **doesn't live** with her family.*
> ***Does** Mei Li **like** the circus? Yes, she **does**.*
> *Where **does** Mei Li **live**?*

Positive		Negative		
He	....	He		live
She	....	She	(does not)	watch
It	**likes**	It		like

Yes/No questions	Short answers
.... he/she/it **live** in China?	Yes, he/she/it **does**.
.... he/she/it **like** animals?	No, he/she/it **doesn't**.

Grammar reference: Workbook page 84

Check it out!

have got

● Don't use *do* with *have got*.
  *He/She/It**'s (has) got** a pet.*
  *He/She/It **hasn't (has not) got** a pet.*
  ***Has** he/she/it **got** a pet?*
  *Yes, he/she/it **has**.   No, he/she/it **hasn't**.*

---

b Write the verbs in the table. Use the text in Exercise 3a to help you.

> finish   like   ~~lives~~   miss   play   speak   teach
> think   ~~watches~~   write

Verb + *-s*	Verb + *-es*
lives	watches ....
....	....

c Complete the words.

1 She love............ school.
2 He do............ like football, but he like............ tennis.
3 Do............ he get up early?
4 She watch............ TV after school.

d Complete the sentences with the correct form of the verbs.

> give   go   not walk   play   teach

1 Her uncle .... English at our school.
2 When .... your cousin .... football?
3 My family .... to the cinema every Sunday.
4 .... your teacher .... you homework every day?
5 Your brother .... to school, he goes by bus.

---

e Use the verbs to write sentences about the people in your family.

> *My sister plays computer games at the weekend.*
> *My grandfather doesn't like …*

> have   like   live   play   speak   watch

⑤ Pronunciation ▶DVD

/s/ and /z/

a 🔊 **1.17** The *-s* at the end of verbs can be pronounced /s/ or /z/. Listen to the examples.

/s/	like**s**	speak**s**
/z/	i**s**	sing**s**

b 🔊 **1.18** Listen and tick (✓) the correct column.

	/s/	/z/
does		
gets up		
goes		
has		
lives		
looks		
plays		
starts		

c 🔊 **1.19** Listen and check. Listen again and repeat.

d 🔊 **1.20** Listen and repeat.

> *She speaks Chinese on Saturdays and sings songs on Sundays.*

6 Vocabulary

School subjects

a 🔊 1.21 Match the words with the pictures. Then listen and check.

1 Art **2** English **3** French **4** Geography **5** History
6 ICT (Information and Communication Technology)
7 Maths **8** Music **9** PE (Physical Education)
10 Science

A

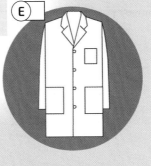

B

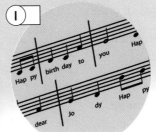

E

F

C

D

I

J

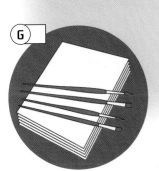

G

H

b Do you know any more school subjects? Write them down.

c Work with a partner. Ask and answer the questions.

1 Which subjects in Exercise 6a do you do at school?
2 What's your favourite subject?
3 What's your favourite school day? Why?

d Write a timetable for your favourite school day.

Monday	
8:40–9:00	Registration
9:00–9:40	English
9:40–10:20	Maths
10:20–11:00	History
11:00–11:20	Break
11:20–12:00	Science
12:00–12:40	Science
12:40–14:10	Lunch
14:10–14:50	French
14:50–15:30	Art

7 Listen

a 🔊 1.22 Listen to Chris. What's his favourite day of the week?

b 🔊 1.22 Listen again and (circle) the correct words.

Morning
School subjects: Geography /
History / French / German

Lunchtime
Help with school magazine / newspaper

Afternoon
School subjects: ICT / PE / Music / Art

After School
Play tennis / football

Evening
Go out with family / friends
Sometimes go to the cinema / swimming pool

⑧ Grammar

Adverbs of frequency

a Look at the table about Megan's week at school and (circle) the adverbs of frequency.

Megan's week at school	Mon	Tues	Wed	Thurs	Fri
She (always) has breakfast.	✓	✓	✓	✓	✓
She usually walks to school.	✓	✓		✓	✓
She's never late for school.					
She often plays basketball after school.	✓			✓	✓
She hardly ever watches TV.				✓	
She sometimes has Maths.		✓		✓	

Grammar reference: Workbook page 84

b Put the adverbs of frequency in order.

~~always~~ hardly ever never often sometimes usually

0% ➔ 100%

_____ _____ _____ _____ _____ *always*

c Put the words in the correct order.

1 have / We / on / always / Wednesdays / PE

_____

2 never / her / does / She / homework

_____

3 online / They / go / hardly ever

_____

4 school / 8:30am / usually / at / at / He / is

_____

d Rewrite the sentences with adverbs from Exercise 8b and make them true for you.

1 My English teacher gives us homework.

_____

2 I go to school on Sundays.

_____

3 We have Science on Tuesdays.

_____

4 My friend is late for school.

_____

5 I go out with my friends on Saturdays.

_____

Check it out!

Adverbs of frequency

- The position of adverbs changes with the verb *be*.
  He **sometimes plays** the guitar.
  (adverb + verb)
  I **am sometimes** late for school.
  (verb be + adverb)

Interaction 2 DVD

Asking about routines

a 🔊 **1.23** Listen to the interview with Jack and tick (✓) the correct answers.

How often do you ... ?	usually	(very) often	sometimes	hardly ever	never
get up early					
read a magazine					
listen to music					
go out with your friends					

b 🔊 **1.23** Listen again and check your answers.

c Work with a partner.
Student A: Turn to page 120.
Student B: Turn to page 122.

Portfolio 2

A letter to a penfriend

a Read the letter about Mika's typical Sunday and match the pictures with the paragraphs.

Hi Emily,

1 ☐ How are you? Thanks for your letter. You ask about my typical Sunday. I always get up late, at about 10 o'clock, and have breakfast. I often do my homework in the morning because we usually have a lot of homework in Japan. Then I go for a walk with my dog, Koro. He's really big, but very friendly!

2 ☐ We usually have lunch at home — my mother, my father, my brother (Hiroshi) and me. We usually have rice or noodles. Noodles are similar to pasta. After lunch I send messages and photos to my friends on my mobile.

3 ☐ In the afternoon, I often go out with my friends. We go to the park and chat. Sometimes I stay at home and play computer games with my brother or watch a DVD.

4 ☐ In the evening, I finish my homework or listen to music. I also go online and write emails to my friends (sometimes in English!) on my laptop. I always go to bed early, at about 10 o'clock.

What about you?
What do you usually do on Sundays?
That's all for now,
Mika

b Write the phrases in the correct columns.

| That's all for now   Hi   See you soon |
| Dear John   Bye   Write soon   Hello   Love |

Start a letter	Finish a letter
....	....
....	....
....	....
	....
	....

c Write a letter to a penfriend about your typical Sunday. Use the text in Exercise a to help you. Write about what you do:

- in the morning
- at lunchtime
- in the afternoon
- in the evening

Review ① and ②

① Grammar

a Complete the sentences with the verbs in the present simple.

> start   not watch   have got   have not got
> speak   not do

1 You _____ a nice dog.
2 I _____ any brothers or sisters, but I've got five cousins.
3 We _____ TV in the summer, we play games in the park.
4 I _____ homework on Wednesday evenings.
5 We _____ French and Italian.
6 They _____ school at 8am.

☐ 6

b (Circle) the correct words.

1 My brother *walk / walks* to school with his friends.
2 Sophie *don't / doesn't* like football.
3 *Do / Does* he speak German?
4 Our teachers *give / gives* us homework every day.
5 She *go / goes* to school in London.
6 My mum and dad *don't / doesn't* work on Saturdays.

☐ 6

c Look at Jim's school week. Complete the sentences. Use adverbs of frequency.

Jim's school week

	Mon	Tues	Wed	Thurs	Fri
walks to school	✓	✓	✓	✓	✓
plays football	✓	✓		✓	✓
plays the guitar	✓		✓		✓
has Science		✓		✓	
is late for school			✓		
goes to the cinema					

1 Jim _____ walks to school.
2 He _____ plays football after school.
3 He _____ plays the guitar.
4 He _____ has Science.
5 He is _____ late for school.
6 He _____ goes to the cinema.

☐ 6

d Complete the questions with the verbs in the present simple.

1 When _____ they _____ (finish) school?
2 What subjects _____ you _____ (study)?
3 What sports _____ they _____ (do) at school?
4 _____ you _____ (like) Maths?
5 Where _____ they _____ (live)?
6 Who _____ you _____ (sit) next to at school?

☐ 6

e Read the letter from George. Choose the correct answer: A, B or C.

> Dear Sergio,
> How ¹ _____ you? ² _____ you want to know about a typical day at my school? I always ³ _____ to school with my brother and my friend Steve. School starts at 8:45. ⁴ _____ the morning we have five lessons – usually different subjects. Then we have lunch. I ⁵ _____ have lunch at school, I go home. In the afternoon there ⁶ _____ two lessons. My favourite subject is Geography. After school we often play football. What about you?
> Bye for now,
> George

1	**A** do	**B** go	**C** are
2	**A** Does	**B** Do	**C** Are
3	**A** walk	**B** walks	**C** walking
4	**A** On	**B** In	**C** At
5	**A** don't	**B** not	**C** doesn't
6	**A** have	**B** is	**C** are

☐ 6

How are you doing?

How many points have you got? Put two crosses on the chart: one for grammar and one for vocabulary.

	1	2	3	4	5	6	7	8	9	10	11	12	13
Grammar													

	1	2	3	4	5	6	7	8	9	10	11	12	13
Vocabulary													

② Vocabulary

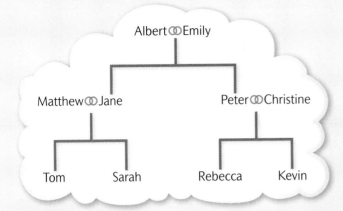

Albert ⚭ Emily

Matthew ⚭ Jane   Peter ⚭ Christine

Tom   Sarah   Rebecca   Kevin

a Complete the sentences with the words.

> brother   mother   sister   cousin   father
> grandfather   aunt   grandmother   uncle

1 Christine is Kevin's ....
2 Tom is Sarah's ....
3 Matthew is Sarah's ....
4 Jane is Rebecca's ....
5 Peter is Tom's ....
6 Rebecca is Kevin's ....
7 Kevin is Sarah's ....
8 Emily is Rebecca's ....
9 Albert is Tom's ....

☐ 9

b Put the letters in the correct order and make seven words.

1 nwspeapre   ....
2 bllrmeau   ....
3 ccklo   ....
4 mrcaae   ....
5 ccbylie   ....
6 skye   ....
7 pmla   ....

☐ 7

c Circle the correct words.

1 In the morning I *get up / go to bed* at 7 am.
2 At 7:45 I have *lunch / breakfast* with Mum and Dad.
3 I *go to / finish* school at 8:15.
4 After school, I *make / do* my homework.
5 Sometimes I *play / have* computer games or go online.
6 I often *listen to / watch* music in the evening.
7 On Fridays I *have got / go out* with my friends.

☐ 7

d Match the sentences (1–7) with the school subjects (A–G).

1 'Moscow is the capital of Russia.'
2 'Turn on your computers and go online.'
3 'How do we spell "umbrella"?'
4 'This song is beautiful. Listen to …'
5 'In the year 1812, Napoleon …'
6 'Water is H_2O. That's hydrogen …'
7 'Are you ready? Everybody run …'

A Music
B Science
C Geography
D ICT
E PE
F History
G English

☐ 7

Correct it!

Correct these typical learner errors from Units 1 and 2.

1 I allways use my car.
   ....

2 It's a very intresting book.
   ....

3 They have five years old.
   ....

4 I fine. How are you?
   ....

5 It's has got a lot of pictures.
   ....

6 I go often to the cinema.
   ....

7 My TV has got three years old.
   ....

8 I don't to have time to listen to music.
   ....

9 My sisters' dress is pretty.
   ....

10 It's five year old and is 500 pesos.
   ....

GREEN: Great! Tell your teacher your score!
YELLOW: Not bad, but go to the website for extra practice.
RED: Talk to your teacher and look at Units 1 and 2 again. Go to the website for extra practice.

14	15	16	17	18	19	20	21	22	23	24	25	26	27	28	29	30

14	15	16	17	18	19	20	21	22	23	24	25	26	27	28	29	30

3 Home and away

Present continuous
Present simple and present continuous
Vocabulary: Holiday activities; Weather and temperature
Interaction 3: Describing a picture

1 Read and listen

a Look at the pictures. Tick (✓) the activities you think you can do at computer camp.

b Read the text quickly and check your answers to Exercise 1a.

go to the beach ☐

do a lot of different sports ☐

meet teenagers from all over the world ☐

make films ☐

go to the shopping centre ☐

play computer games ☐

COMPUTER CAMP

Is computer camp fun? We talk to two teenagers, Luke and Molly, who are there right now.

What are you learning about computers?

Luke: I'm learning a lot of new things like webpage design. My friend Alex and I are also designing a computer game.

Molly: I'm learning how to make films with computers and digital cameras. My class is making a short film about summer in the USA.

Are the other campers and the teachers nice?

Luke: Everybody's great. I'm making lots of friends. There are people here from lots of different countries, not just the USA, but we all speak English together. The teachers are nice too.

Molly: Yeah, they're great! I'm sharing a room with two girls, Rosie and Tina. Rosie is American, like me, and Tina is British. Poor Tina, she isn't enjoying the camp and she wants to go home.

What do you do after class?

Luke: In the afternoons I do lots of sport. I'm teaching the Americans in my class to play football, or soccer. They're teaching me to play American football, which is very different from the football we play in Britain!

Molly: After class I usually go for a walk. It's beautiful here and it's always sunny. On Saturday evenings I go to the disco with my friends and we sometimes do karaoke.

c 🔊 1.25 Read the text again and listen. Then answer the questions. Write *M* (Molly), *L* (Luke) or *B* (both Molly and Luke).

1 Who is making a computer game? ....
2 Who is making a film? ....
3 Who likes the camp? ....
4 Who likes the teachers? ....
5 Who does sport in the afternoon? ....
6 Who is learning a new sport? ....
7 Who dances at the weekend? ....
8 Who is American? ....
9 Who is British? ....

Culture Vulture

Did you know that 10 million children in the USA go to summer camp each year? Do children in your country go to summer camp?

2 Grammar Present continuous

a Look at the examples and complete the table.

> *I'm learning a lot of new things.*
> *She isn't enjoying the camp.*
> *We're designing a computer game.*
>
> *What are you learning about computers?*
> *Are they designing a webpage?   Yes, they are.*

Positive

I	.... **(am)**	
He/She/It	.... **(is)**	work**ing**
You/We/They	.... **(are)**	

Negative

I	'm not **(am not)**	
He/She/It	.... **(is not)**	work**ing**
You/We/They	aren't **(are not)**	

Yes/No questions

Am	I	
Is	he/she/it	work**ing**?
....	you/we/they	

Short answers

Yes, I **am**.	No, I'**m not**.
Yes, he/she/it **is**.	No, he/she/it **isn't**.
Yes, you/we/they	No, you/we/they **aren't**.

Information questions

What **are** you **learning** about computers?

Answers

I'**m** learn**ing** a lot.

(Circle) the correct word(s) to complete the rule.

● We use the present continuous for actions happening **now** / **every day** and for temporary actions.

Grammar reference: Workbook page 86

b 🔊 **1.26** Correct the sentences about the pictures. Then listen and check.

1 They're talking.

They aren't talking. They're writing.

2 She's doing her homework.

---

3 They're making a film.

---

4 We're reading magazines.

---

5 He's getting dressed.

---

6 They're playing tennis.

Check it out!

Spelling of -ing verbs

The spelling of verbs changes in the present continuous.

● Verbs ending in -e (*write, make*) → e + -ing: *write → writing*

● Verbs ending in -ie (*lie*) → ie + -ying: *lie → lying.*

● Short verbs ending in a vowel + a consonant → double the consonant: *swim → swimming*

c Write sentences about what these people are doing at the moment.

> I   My teacher
>   My friend   My ...

> write   work   learn English
>   speak English   read   play ...

> *I'm writing. My friend isn't working.*

③ Vocabulary

Holiday activities

a 🔊 1.27 Match the words with the pictures. Then listen and check.

> **1** buy souvenirs **2** go camping
> **3** go to a disco **4** have an ice cream
> **5** play games **6** ride a horse **7** sunbathe
> **8** surf **9** swim **10** take photos

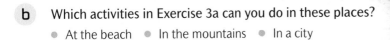

b Which activities in Exercise 3a can you do in these places?
- At the beach
- In the mountains
- In a city

c Do you know any more holiday activities? Where can you do them? Write them down.

④ Speak

a Write another answer for each question in the quiz.

Holiday Quiz

1 Where do you usually go on holiday?
  A the beach B a city C a campsite D ....

2 When do you usually go on holiday?
  A in summer B in winter C in summer and winter D in ....

3 What do you sometimes do on holiday?
  A sunbathe B surf C buy souvenirs D ....

4 What do you never do on holiday?
  A go camping B go to a disco C take photos D ....

b Work with a partner. Ask and answer the questions in the quiz. Write your partner's answers.

> A: *Where do you usually go on holiday?*
> B: *The beach.*

⑤ Pronunciation DVD

Word stress

a 🔊 1.28 Listen to the words and <u>underline</u> the stressed syllable.

> <u>foot</u>ball <u>a</u>bout making
> mountain enjoy decide
> photo because

b Write the words in Exercise 5a in the correct column.

●●	●●
football	about

c 🔊 1.29 Listen and check. Listen again and repeat.

6 Listen

a 🔊 1.30 Listen to three teenagers talking about their holidays. Match the people with the places.

1 Lucy   **A** in the mountains
2 Paolo   **B** on the beach
3 Erin   **C** in a city

b 🔊 1.30 Listen again and match the people with the activities. Write *L* (Lucy), *P* (Paolo) or *E* (Erin).

7 Grammar

Present simple and present continuous

a Look at the examples. Which are present simple and which are present continuous? Write *PS* or *PC*.

⟶ *I'm buying* souvenirs for my friends at home. ....
Every day we go to the beach and we meet our friends. ....
We're drinking hot chocolate and playing games. ....
I love Thailand! ....

Circle the correct words to complete the rules.

- We use the **present simple** / **present continuous** to talk about things in general. We use it to say that something happens all the time, not just now.
- We use the **present simple** / **present continuous** for actions happening now.

Grammar reference: Workbook pages 84, 86

Check it out!

State verbs

- Don't use *like*, *love*, *hate*, *want*, *know*, *understand* in the present continuous.

b Circle the correct words.

1 This week he's *learning / learns* how to design computer games.
2 In the summer I*'m sunbathing / sunbathe* at the swimming pool.
3 What *is she doing / does she do* at the moment?
4 I can't talk now, I*'m having / have* dinner.
5 *Are you watching / Do you watch* TV right now?
6 We*'re staying / stay* at the beach every summer.

c Work with a partner. Ask and answer the questions.

1 What language do you usually speak with your family?
2 What language are you speaking at the moment?
3 What music do you usually listen to?
4 What music are you listening to at the moment?
5 Who are you sitting next to right now?
6 Who do you usually sit next to at dinner?

(8) Vocabulary

Weather and temperature

a 🔊 **1.31** Complete the sentences with the words. Then listen and check.

> cloudy   foggy   rainy   snowy   sunny   windy

1 It's ....   **2** It's ....

3 It's ....   **4** It's ....

5 It's ....   **6** It's ....

b 🔊 **1.32** Listen and answer the questions. Then listen and check.

c Write the words in the correct place.

> It's freezing.   It's cold.   It's cool.
> It's hot.   It's really hot.   It's warm.

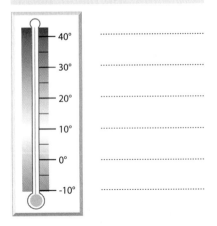

d Work with a partner. Ask and answer the questions.

1 What's the weather like in your country today?

2 What's the weather like in your country in spring/ summer/autumn/winter?

3 What's your favourite type of weather?

Interaction 3 DVD

Describing a picture

a 🔊 **1.33** Listen to Joe and Rebecca comparing their pictures. Look at Joe's picture. How many differences do they find?

b 🔊 **1.33** Listen again and match the two parts of the sentences.

1 What's the weather

2 What are people

3 In my picture there are

4 How many people are

5 There isn't

6 That's

A two boys and two girls.

B playing tennis in your picture?

C like in your picture?

D doing in your picture?

E another difference.

F a girl in my picture.

c Work with a partner.

Student A: Turn to page 120.
Student B: Turn to page 122.

Portfolio 3

A postcard

a Look at the two postcards and read the sentences. Where is Tom? Where is Daisy?

b Put the four parts of each postcard (1–4 and A–D) in the correct order.

☐ day!
Simon's friends are very friendly but I don't always understand them.
Bye for now.
Tom

☐ very beautiful city. I'm taking lots of photos and buying lots of souvenirs. We're

A Hi Mark
I'm having a great time in France with my penfriend Simon and

☐ raining. In the evenings we go to discos. Prague's fantastic! See you soon.
Daisy

1 Hello Lucy
I'm staying in the centre of Prague with my cousin Sofia. It's a

☐ sea.
It's always sunny and I surf every

☐ his family. His sister Pauline is really nice. We're staying in a house near the

c Look at the postcards and (circle) seven adjectives.

d Imagine you are on holiday. Write a postcard (about 50 words) to a friend. Write about:
- where you're staying
- what the weather's like
- what you're doing

☐ sitting in a lovely café at the moment. We can't go out because it's

Which summer camp is for you?

Millions of North American children and teenagers go to summer camp every year. At traditional camps the 'campers' do outdoor activities, for example, swimming, riding horses or water-skiing. Many camps specialise in one activity – you can learn about ecology, music, science, fashion, and many more things. Check out our selection of camps.

Mountain adventure

Walk and climb in the beautiful North Cascades (Washington State), then camp under the stars next to a lake. You learn about plants and animals and how to survive in the mountains.

Circus camp

Would you like to be in a circus? We've got classes for beginners and advanced students. More than 500 young people come every year and have a fantastic time with us. This year you can come too!

Fashion design

Are you the next Louis Vuitton or Giorgio Armani? Design and make your own clothes, then wear them at the fashion show.

Calling all artists!

Be an artist at our Youth Arts Centre for students aged 13–18. We've got courses in art, dance, music and theatre. Our students have lots of fun and our teachers are excellent.

Whale camp

Come to Grand Manan Island (between USA and Canada) and watch whales. Go round the island in a kayak and take photos of other sea animals and birds. Learn about ecology with marine biologists.

Space camp

Meet NASA scientists and astronauts. Learn how to walk in space. See the stars in the summer sky. Design and build your own rocket.

1 Culture World: USA

a Read the magazine page quickly. Match the summer camps with the activities.

1 painting

2 animals

3 making clothes

....

....

....

4 walking in the country

5 science

6 acrobatics

....

....

....

b Are the sentences *right* (✓) or *wrong* (✗)?

1 A lot of US and Canadian children and teenagers go to summer camp.

2 Campers can do more than one activity at some summer camps.

3 At the Mountain adventure camp you sleep outside.

4 There isn't a camp for people who like dancing.

5 You can go on a boat at the Whale camp.

6 At the Space camp you can go up into space in a rocket.

c Which summer camp would you like to go to? Why?

2 Your project

A summer camp

a Work in a group. Find out about activities you can do in different places in your country in the summer.

Name of place	Name of activity	Information
Paros	Sea kayaking	Sea kayaking is really fun and good exercise too!
Meteora	Hiking and climbing	Many advanced climbers go to Meteora.

b Draw a map of your country and put the information on your map.

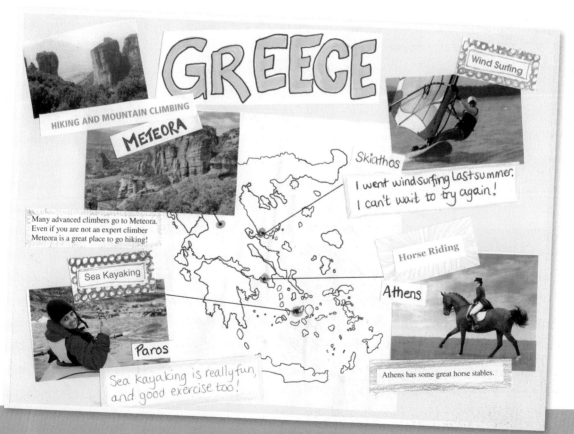

4 Sport crazy

Verb + -*ing*
Adverbs of manner
Vocabulary: Sports; Sports words
Interaction 4: Making decisions

1 Read and listen

a Read the text quickly and (circle) all the sports.

Football mad at sports college

Do you like playing sports like basketball and hockey, or doing athletics? Would you like to have expert sports teachers? Yes? Then how about going to a sports college?

There are more than 300 special sports colleges in Britain. Brandon is 15 and goes to a sports college in London. Students study the same subjects as in normal schools but they do a lot of sport. In PE classes, Brandon plays rugby, volleyball, cricket and goes swimming. 'I enjoy doing a lot of different sports,' he says, 'but my favourite is football. I love football.

'I really like going to a sports college because our teachers are professional sportsmen and women and they're all really nice. We sometimes travel to different countries, but I hate getting up early to go to the airport. At the moment my football teacher is organising a tour of Italy.'

Brandon plays in Chelsea Football Club's under-16 team.

He sometimes meets famous players at Stamford Bridge, Chelsea's football stadium. His favourite players are Maradona and Ronaldinho.

What about school subjects that are not sport? 'I like doing Art,' Brandon says, 'but I don't like doing homework after school. I just want to play football.'

Culture Vulture

Did you know that the five most popular sports in British schools are football, dance, gymnastics, athletics and cricket? What sports do you do at your school? What sports do you like?

b 🔊 1.34 Read the text again and listen. Are the sentences *right* (✓), *wrong* (✗) or *doesn't say* (–)?

1 Brandon goes to a normal school. ☐
2 At sports colleges the students don't study normal school subjects. ☐
3 Brandon likes his school. ☐
4 Brandon is in Italy at the moment. ☐
5 Brandon's football teacher is Italian. ☐
6 Chelsea Football Club plays at Stamford Bridge. ☐
7 Brandon likes David Beckham. ☐
8 Brandon likes doing school work in the evening. ☐

2 Vocabulary

Sports

a 🔊 **1.35** Match the words with the pictures. Then listen and check.

1 athletics	**2** basketball	**3** cricket	**4** cycling	**5** football
6 hockey	**7** judo	**8** rugby	**9** skiing	**10** swimming
11 tennis	**12** volleyball			

A

B

C

D

E

F

G

H

I

J

K

L

b Do you know any more sports? Write them down.

c 🔊 **1.36** Listen to the sounds. Which sports from Exercise 2a can you hear?

d Complete the table with the sports in Exercise 2a.

Individual sports	Team sports
athletics	basketball

3 Speak

a Put the words in the correct order.

1 Which / you / do / sports / at / do / school ?

....

....

2 do / When / do / you / sport ?

....

....

3 favourite / are / your / Who / sports stars ?

....

....

4 do / you / go / How often / running ?

....

....

5 team / sports / play / you / Do ?

....

....

6 What / TV / you / do / on / sports / watch ?

....

....

7 football / is / What / favourite / your / team ?

....

....

8 swimming / you / do / go / How often ?

....

....

b Work with a partner. Ask and answer the questions in Exercise 3a.

(4) Grammar

Verb + -ing

a Look at the examples. Then (circle) the correct words to complete the rules.

> ⋯⋗ I **enjoy** doing a lot of different sports.
> I **hate** getting up early to go to the airport.
> I **don't like** doing homework after school.
> Do you **like** playing basketball?
> My favourite is football. I **love** football.

- After the verbs *like*, *love*, *hate* and *enjoy*, we use **the infinitive** / **verb + -ing**.
- After the verbs *like*, *love*, *hate* and *enjoy*, we can use **a noun** / **an adverb**.

Grammar reference: Workbook page 88

Check it out!

really + verb
- **really** can be used before a verb for emphasis.
  He **really likes** playing tennis.
  He **likes** playing tennis .

b Complete the sentences with the words in the box.

don't like   like/enjoy   hate   love

1 I .... playing tennis.

2 I .... / ....
playing tennis.

3 I .... playing tennis.

4 I .... playing tennis.

c 🔊 1.37 Complete the sentences with the verb + -ing. Then listen and check.

do   go   play   ski   swim   watch

1 Jess loves .... judo.
2 They enjoy .... the Olympics on TV.
3 We really like .... in the Alps in February.
4 Sam hates .... rugby but he likes football.
5 I don't like .... in the pool at the sports centre.
6 Do you like .... running in the morning?

d Write sentences about your partner. Use *love*, *enjoy*, *like*, *don't like* and *hate*.

- speak English
- do homework
- go shopping
- listen to music
- clean your room
- get up early
- go out with friends
- write emails

⋯⋗ He really likes getting up early.

e Now show your partner the sentences. Are they correct?

(5) Pronunciation ⊙D•D

/ŋ/

a 🔊 1.38 Listen to the /ŋ/ sound at the end of these words.

swimming   cycling   skiing   surfing

b Match the phonetics with the words.

1 /lɒŋ/   **A** finger
2 /fɪŋgə/   **B** raining
3 /hʌngriː/   **C** sing
4 /rʌnɪŋ/   **D** hungry
5 /sɪŋ/   **E** long
6 /sɒŋ/   **F** going
7 /gəʊɪŋ/   **G** running
8 /reɪnɪŋ/   **H** song

c 🔊 1.39 Listen and check. Listen again and repeat.

d 🔊 1.40 Listen and repeat.

The hungry singer likes singing long songs.

⑥ Vocabulary

Sports words

a 🔊 **1.41** Match the words with the pictures. Then listen and check.

> **1** bounce the ball   **2** catch the ball   **3** hit the ball
> **4** kick the ball   **5** pick up the ball   **6** throw the ball

A

B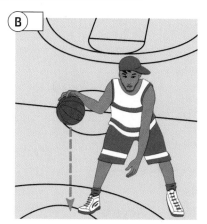

C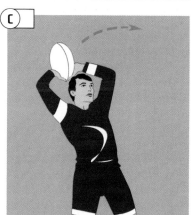

D

E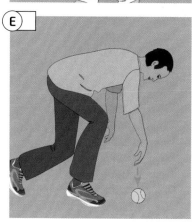

F

b What do you do with the ball in these sports?

> basketball   hockey   tennis   football   volleyball   rugby

c Work with a partner. Describe a sport in Exercise 2a. Can your partner guess the sport?

A: *You kick the ball and one person can catch the ball.*
B: *Football.*

⑦ Listen

a 🔊 **1.42** Listen to four teenagers talking about the sports they do. Write the sports next to their names.

Keiko   ....
Juma   ....
Nadja   ....
Dieter   ....

b 🔊 **1.42** Listen again. Are the sentences *right* (✓) or *wrong* (✗)?

1 Keiko does her sport in the evening. ☐

2 Juma's friends watch him do his sport. ☐

3 Nadja plays her sport in competitions. ☐

4 Dieter's sport is easy. ☐

8 Grammar Adverbs of manner

a Read the text and complete the table with the adverbs in **bold**.

Rafael Nadal is an excellent tennis player, but he is good at other sports too. He plays football **well** and he enjoys playing golf.

Rafael travels around the world playing tennis and he speaks lots of English. He says that he speaks English **badly**. He doesn't understand people when they speak **quickly** or **quietly**.

Rafael is always happy. 'It's very important to enjoy life,' he says!

Check it out!

To be good / bad at …
- He's **bad at** speaking French.
  = He speaks French badly.
- I'm **good at** football.
  = I play football well.

Regular		Irregular	
Adjective	**Adverb**	**Adjective**	**Adverb**
bad	....	early	early
quick	....	fast	fast
quiet	....	good	....
slow	slowly	hard	hard
		late	late
Adjective ending in -y			
easy	easily		
noisy	noisily		

Circle the correct words to complete the rules.
- We use **adverbs** / **adjectives** to describe a noun.
- We use **adverbs** / **adjectives** to describe a verb.

Grammar reference: Workbook page 88

b Write the adverbs for these adjectives.

1 careful ....
2 happy ....
3 sad ....
4 loud ....

c 🔊 1.43 Listen and circle the correct adverbs.

1 He's walking *slowly / fast.*
2 She's talking *loudly / quietly.*
3 He's playing the violin *well / badly.*
4 She's eating *quickly / quietly.*
5 He's driving *carefully / fast.*
6 She's singing *happily / sadly.*

d Work with a partner. Take it in turns to give different instructions and follow them.

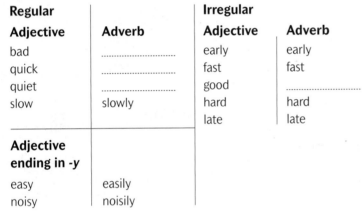

speak English
write your name
say the English alphabet
read a book

quickly quietly
loudly badly sadly
slowly happily fast
well

⤳ *Say the English alphabet quickly.*

Interaction 4 DVD

Making decisions

a 🔊 1.44 Asif and Rob are at the sports centre. Listen and circle the sport they decide to do.

Fitness SPORTS CENTRE

GET FIT, DO MORE SPORT!

judo	tennis
swimming	football
rugby	volleyball
basketball	athletics

b 🔊 1.44 Listen again and complete the sentences.

1 I really like ....
2 What about ....?
3 I don't ....
4 What about ....?
5 What are you ....?
6 But I'm .... catching.
7 Hmm, ...!

c Work with a partner.

Student A: Turn to page 120.
Student B: Turn to page 122.

Portfolio 4

An email

a Read the email. Where does Olivia live? Where does Amy live?

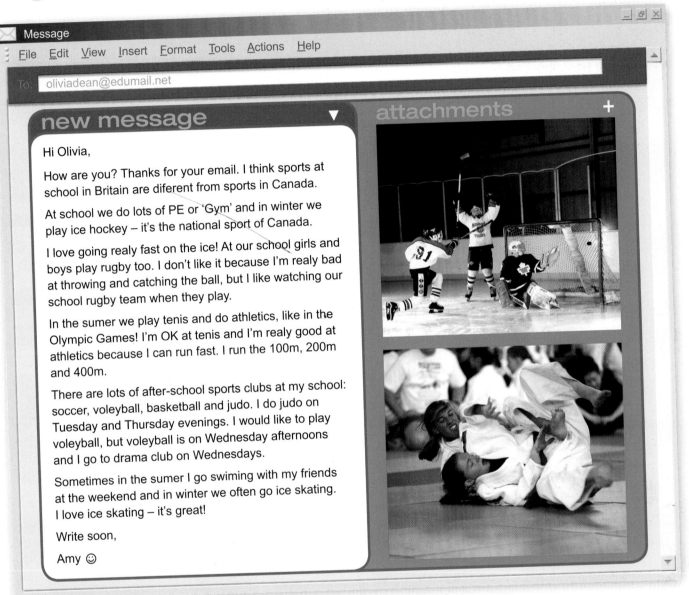

Message

File Edit View Insert Format Tools Actions Help

To: oliviadean@edumail.net

new message ▼   **attachments** +

Hi Olivia,

How are you? Thanks for your email. I think sports at school in Britain are diferent from sports in Canada.

At school we do lots of PE or 'Gym' and in winter we play ice hockey – it's the national sport of Canada.

I love going realy fast on the ice! At our school girls and boys play rugby too. I don't like it because I'm really bad at throwing and catching the ball, but I like watching our school rugby team when they play.

In the sumer we play tenis and do athletics, like in the Olympic Games! I'm OK at tenis and I'm realy good at athletics because I can run fast. I run the 100m, 200m and 400m.

There are lots of after-school sports clubs at my school: soccer, voleyball, basketball and judo. I do judo on Tuesday and Thursday evenings. I would like to play voleyball, but voleyball is on Wednesday afternoons and I go to drama club on Wednesdays.

Sometimes in the sumer I go swiming with my friends at the weekend and in winter we often go ice skating. I love ice skating – it's great!

Write soon,

Amy ☺

b Six different words in the email are wrongly spelt. Can you correct them?

c Complete the table with the sports in the email.

Amy's school sports	
Winter	ice hockey, rugby ....
Summer	....
After-school clubs	....

d Write an email to a friend about the sports at your school and the sports you do. Use the email and the words in Exercise c to help you. Write about:
- the sports you do at school
- the sports you like / don't like
- the sports you're good at / bad at

e Check your email for spelling mistakes.

Happy Days

1 Song

a Work with a partner. Write the days of the week in the correct order.

b 🔊 **1.45** Listen to part of the song and choose the correct option.

1.
Monday, Tuesday, happy days.
Wednesday, Thursday, happy days.
Friday, Saturday, happy days.

2.
Sunday, Monday, happy days.
Tuesday, Wednesday, happy days.
Thursday, Friday, happy days.

3.
Friday, Saturday, happy days.
Sunday, Monday, happy days.
Tuesday, Wednesday, happy days.

c Complete the table with the words.

blue   free   long   me   wrong   you

/uː/	/iː/	/ɒ/
who	be	hot

d 🔊 **1.46** Listen to and complete the song.

These days are all
Happy and ¹_____ . (Those happy days)
These days are all
Share them with ²_____ . (Oh baby)
Goodbye grey skies, hello ³_____ .
There's nothing can hold me when
    I hold ⁴_____ .
You're so right, you can't be ⁵_____ .
Rockin' and rollin' all week ⁶_____ .

e Work with a partner and answer the questions about the song.

1. Which days of the week are happy days?
2. What colour is the sky on a happy day?
3. Why do you think the singer is happy?

f Which days of the week are happy days for you? Why?

② Sound check

a 🔊 **1.47** Listen and match the lines to the correct stress pattern, A or B.

1 Sunday, Monday, happy days. ....
2 Happy and free. ....

Ⓐ ● ● ● ●   Ⓑ ● ● ● ● ● ● ●

b 🔊 **1.48** Match the lines with the correct stress pattern: A or B. Then listen and check.

1 Those happy days. ....
2 Goodbye grey skies, hello blue. ....
3 Feels so right, it can't be wrong. ....
4 Tuesday, Wednesday, happy days ....
5 Thursday, Friday, happy days. ....
6 Share them with me. ....

③ Musical notes

The song *Happy Days* is from an American TV programme about life in the 1950s and 1960s. The type of music is rock and roll but there are also lots of other types of music from this time.

a 🔊 **1.49** Listen to the extracts. Write the names of each type of music.

1 .... 3 ....
2 .... 4 ....

b Do you know any types of music from the 1950s and 1960s in your country?

Doo wop

Country

Rock and roll

Jive

Review ③ and ④

① Grammar

a

Complete the sentences with the verbs in the present continuous.

> have   listen   not watch   read   speak   play

1 Right now John .... basketball with the school team.
2 .... Mary .... breakfast? It's time to go to school.
3 Andy and Amy .... a DVD. They're playing computer games.
4 Which CD .... you .... to?
5 Please be quiet! I .... my book.
6 What language .... she ....?

☐ 6

b

Put the words in the correct order.

1 my / I / doing / homework / hate

....
....

2 to / cinema / They / going / like / the

....
....

3 watching / don't / We / TV / like

....
....

4 like / sister / reading / doesn't / My / magazines

....
....

5 dad / music / hates / My / to / listening / country

....
....

6 enjoy / on / They / photos / taking / holiday

....
....

☐ 6

c

Complete the sentences with the verbs in the present simple or the present continuous.

1 We .... (play) tennis now.
2 Right now we .... (speak) Spanish.
3 I sometimes .... (play) the guitar in a band.
4 When .... Susie usually .... (do) her homework?
5 I .... (not understand) Italian.
6 .... they .... (like) chocolate ice cream?

☐ 6

d

Complete the sentences with adverbs.

1 Look at him! He's walking very .... (quick).
2 He plays the piano very .... (good).
3 Please talk .... (quiet)!
4 I speak German very .... (bad).
5 Can you speak .... (slow), please?
6 We're working .... (hard) today.

☐ 6

e

Complete the six conversations. Choose the correct answer: A, B or C.

1 What are you doing?
   A I often watch TV.
   B I'm doing my homework.
   C I like listening to music.

2 I enjoy playing tennis.
   A I don't like reading.
   B Where do you play?
   C In the afternoons.

3 It's sunny today.
   A I like camping.
   B How much is the ticket?
   C Yes. Do you want to go to the beach?

4 I love football.
   A What's your favourite team?
   B Do you like football?
   C I'm watching the match.

5 Can you pick up the ball, please?
   A I play rugby on Tuesdays.
   B Yes, of course I do.
   C Yes, here you are.

6 He speaks English very well.
   A Can you speak more slowly, please?
   B I don't understand the question.
   C Yes. His mother's American.

☐ 6

How are you doing?

How many points have you got? Put two crosses on the chart: one for grammar and one for vocabulary.

2 Vocabulary

a Complete the sentences with the words.

> buy souvenirs go camping go to a disco swim
> have an ice cream play games take photos

1 When we _____ we sleep in a tent.
2 Do you want to _____ and dance?
3 He can _____ with his new camera.
4 It's hot! I want to _____ in the sea.
5 Would you like to _____? The chocolate ones are good.
6 I sometimes _____ like table tennis.
7 You can _____ at the shop in the town.

`7`

b Look at the map. Complete the sentences with the words.

> cloudy cold foggy freezing rainy sunny warm

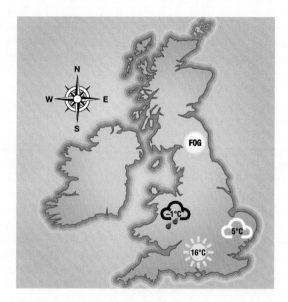

1 In the west it's _____ and _____ .
2 In the south it's _____ and _____ .
3 In the east it's _____ and _____ .
4 In the north it's _____ .

`7`

c Find ten more sports in the puzzle.

G	S	O	D	U	J	H	T	L	B
N	R	C	X	L	O	K	L	A	C
I	U	U	I	C	W	A	S	G	R
M	G	P	K	T	B	K	N	H	I
M	B	E	J	T	E	I	X	J	C
I	Y	L	O	T	I	L	T	F	K
W	D	O	B	K	E	Q	H	X	E
S	F	A	S	I	N	N	E	T	T
L	L	C	Y	C	L	I	N	G	A
L	L	A	B	Y	E	L	L	O	V

`10`

d Complete the sentences with the words.

> throw hit kick bounce catch pick up

1 In basketball you _____ the ball on the floor.
2 In tennis you _____ the ball.
3 In football you _____ the ball.
4 In rugby you _____ the ball to people in your team.
5 In football the goalkeeper needs to _____ the ball.
6 In hockey you never _____ the ball.

`6`

Correct it!

Correct these typical learner errors from Units 3 and 4.

1 Do you like play football?
....

2 I am writting to you from my new house in London.
....

3 She is like singing and reading books.
....

4 At the moment I staying in Russia.
....

5 The weather is raining today.
....

6 I am loving ice cream.
....

7 I don't enjoying films.
....

8 I love driving fastly.
....

9 The weather are very good.
....

10 I like lisening to music.
....

GREEN: Great! Tell your teacher your score!
YELLOW: Not bad, but go to the website for extra practice.
RED: Talk to your teacher and look at Units 3 and 4 again. Go to the website for extra practice.

14	15	16	17	18	19	20	21	22	23	24	25	26	27	28	29	30

14	15	16	17	18	19	20	21	22	23	24	25	26	27	28	29	30

5 Fame!

Past simple: the verb *be*
Past simple: regular verbs
Vocabulary: Describing people; Jobs
Interaction 5: Describing someone

1 Listen

a 🔊 **1.50** Match the names of the famous people with the pictures. Then listen and check.

1 Angelina Jolie	**2** Kate Moss	
3 Lewis Hamilton	**4** Madonna	
5 Orlando Bloom	**6** Wayne Rooney	

b 🔊 **1.51** Listen to two descriptions of people from Exercise 1a. Who are they?

c 🔊 **1.51** Listen again and complete the table.

Name	Angelina Jolie	**Name**	Lewis Hamilton
Age in photo	about _8 9_ years old	Age in photo	about _10_ years old
Hair colour	_brown_	Hair colour	_short black hair_
Eye colour	_brown_	Eye colour	_brown_
Born (date)	_4th_ June, _1975_	Born (date)	7th _January_, 1985
Born (place)	Los Angeles, _in Unites States_	Born (place)	Stevenage, _in England_

2 Vocabulary Describing people

a Complete the table with the words.

black   blonde   brown x2   slim   curly
long   straight   grey x2   blue   short x2
green   red   wavy   tall

Hair colour	Hairstyle	Eye colour	Body
black	_curly_	_blue_	_Slim_
blond	_long_	_grey_	_Tall_
grey	_straight_	_brown_	_short_
brown	_short_	_green_	
red	_wavy_		

b Do you know any more words to describe people? Write them down.

c Write a description of a person in Exercise 1a.

⤷ *He's got brown hair. He's tall and …*

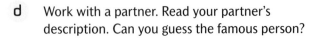

d Work with a partner. Read your partner's description. Can you guess the famous person?

Check it out!

have got* and the verb *be

● Use *have got* and the verb *be* to describe people.
  She's got long red hair. He's got blue eyes. He is tall. She is slim.

(3) Grammar

Past simple: the verb *be*

a Look at the examples and complete the table.

> ⟶ *They **were** about five years old in the photos.*
> *He **was** a short child.*
>
> *She **wasn't** very tall.*
> *Where **was** he born?*

Positive			Negative		
I/He/She/It	....	short.	I/He/She/It	.... / **was not**	tall.
You/We/They	....		You/We/They	**weren't** / **were not**	

Yes/No questions			Short answers	
Was	I/he/she/it	late?	Yes, I/he/she/it **was**.	No, I/he/she/it **wasn't**.
Were	you/we/they		Yes, you/we/they **were**.	No, you/we/they **weren't**.

Information questions				Answers		
Where	**was**	I/he/she/it	born?	I/He/She/It	**was**	born in Paris.
When	**were**	you/we/they	born?	You/We/They	**were**	born in 1985.
Who	**was**	your	favourite actor?	Leonardo DiCaprio.		
What	**were**	your	favourite films?	*The Jungle Book* and *Pinocchio*.		

Circle the correct word to complete the rule.

• We use *was* and *were* to talk about the **past** / **present**.

Grammar reference: Workbook page 90

b Circle the correct words.

1 Ruth *was* / *were* in the park on Saturday.
2 Sadia and James *were* / *was* at the cinema.
3 They *were* / *weren't* at home. They were on holiday.
4 When he *was* / *wasn't* a child his favourite song was *Lose Yourself*.

c Complete the sentences with the past simple of the verb *be*. Use the positive or negative form.

1 Rembrandt .... a Dutch painter.
2 Pierre and Marie Curie .... famous scientists.
3 Kate Winslet .... in *Titanic*.
4 The Beatles .... actors, they .... musicians.
5 Michael Jordan .... born in New York in 1963.
6 Kylie Minogue .... born in the USA – she's Australian.

Culture Vulture

Did you know that 11% of British teenagers want to be famous? Do many teenagers in your country want to be famous? Would you like to be famous? Why / Why not?

d Put the words in the correct order.

1 born / were / Where / you ?
----
2 you / were / When / born ?
----
3 a / Who was / child / when / favourite / your / you / were / singer ?
----
4 films / What were / child / favourite / when / your / you / were / a ?
----
5 were / your / child / sports star / you / Who was / a / favourite / when ?
----
6 when / a / favourite / you / toys / were / child / What were / your ?
----

e Work with a partner. Ask and answer the questions in Exercise 3d.

A: *Where were you born?*
B: *I was born in Madrid.*

(4) Read and listen

a Read the texts quickly and match them with the people.

A — Keira Knightley
B — Lionel Messi
C — Shakira
D — Christopher Paolini

Before they were famous

1 ☐ When he was young he lived in Montana, USA, with his family. His parents didn't want him to go to school so he studied at home with them. He enjoyed reading, especially books about magic and dragons, and he listened to classical music a lot. Beethoven and Mahler's music helped him to write. He started his first book, *Eragon*, at the age of 15.

2 ☐ She was born in Barranquilla, Colombia. She started writing poems when she was four years old. When she was young she wanted to be a dancer but then she decided to be a singer. She recorded her first CD in 1991, at the age of 14, but it wasn't very popular. Things changed in 1995, with her third CD, *Pies Descalzos*. First she was famous in Latin America and then in the USA and Europe. In 2006 she performed at the football World Cup.

3 ☐ He was born in 1987 in Rosario, in Argentina. His father coached the local club and he started to play football when he was five. When he was 13 he moved to Spain with his family to play in the Barcelona youth team. He first played for FC Barcelona when he was 17 and for Argentina when he was 18. He was the number one goal scorer in the Champions' League when Barcelona lifted the trophy in 2009.

4 ☐ She wanted to be an actress at the age of three. Her parents were both actors and she acted on British TV when she was seven. She was in the Hollywood film, *Star Wars: Episode 1 – The Phantom Menace*, when she was 14. A few years later she was in *Bend it Like Beckham*, a famous British film. She was a star at the age of 17.

b 🔊 1.52 Read the texts again and listen. Write *K* (Keira), *L* (Lionel), *S* (Shakira) or *C* (Christopher).

1 .... started to write at the age of four.
2 .... moved to a different country at the age of 13.
3 .... loved music.
4 .... wanted to do the same job as her parents.
5 ....'s parents were his teachers.
6 .... worked in Britain.
7 .... played for his father.
8 .... first worked in the USA at the age of 14.

(5) Vocabulary

Jobs

a 🔊 **1.53** Match the words with the pictures. Then listen and check.

1 actor   2 artist
3 business person
4 dancer   5 model
6 musician
7 photographer
8 singer
9 sports person
10 writer

 A
 B
 C
 D
 E

b 🔊 **1.54** Listen to eight people and write their jobs.

1 He's an ....
2 She's a ....
3 She's a ....
4 He's a ....
5 She's a ....
6 He's a ....
7 She's a ....
8 He's a ....

 F
 G
 H

c Do you know any more jobs? Write them down.

d Which job(s) would you like to do?

 I
 J

(6) Grammar

Past simple: regular verbs

a Look at the examples and complete the table.

⤑ *When he was young he **lived** in Montana, USA, with his family.*
*His parents **didn't want** him to go to school.*
*He **studied** at home with them.*

Positive		Negative		
want → I/You/He/She/It/We/They **wanted**				**want**
live → I/You/He/She/It/We/They	I/You/He/She/It/We/They .... **(did not)**			**live**
study → I/You/He/She/It/We/They **studied**				**study**

(Circle) the correct words to complete the rules.

● If a verb ends in a **consonant** / **vowel** followed by -*y*, make the past simple by changing the -*y* to -*ied*.
● The negative form of the regular past simple is always ***didn't*** + **verb** / ***wasn't*** + **verb**.

Grammar reference: Workbook page 90

b Look at the texts in Exercise 4a. Find 16 different regular past simple verbs.

Check it out!

Past simple negative
● After *didn't* use the infinitive, not the past simple.

c 🔊 **1.55** Read and choose the correct answer: A, B or C. Then listen and check.

Scarlett Johansson was ¹............ in New York City in 1984. She ².......... to be an actress when she ³............ a child and she ⁴............ in the film *North* when she ⁵............ ten years old. As a teenager she ⁶............ to secondary school but she ⁷............ at an acting school in Manhattan. In 2003 she ⁸............ in *Lost in Translation*.

1	**A** born	**B** started	**C** lived
2	**A** were	**B** wanted	**C** was
3	**A** was	**B** wasn't	**C** were
4	**A** studied	**B** liked	**C** acted
5	**A** were	**B** was	**C** acted
6	**A** didn't go	**B** didn't start	**C** didn't finish
7	**A** studied	**B** liked	**C** enjoyed
8	**A** wasn't	**B** weren't	**C** was

b 🔊 **1.57** Listen and check.

c 🔊 **1.58** Listen and repeat.

Yesterday David played football, cooked lunch, listened to music, watched a film, visited a friend and danced all night.

d Write three true and three false sentences about when you were a child. Use the verbs.

like   play   visit   live   hate   study

┄┄⟫ *When I was five, I played the violin.*

e Work with a partner. Read your partner's sentences. Which are true?

7 Pronunciation DVD

Regular past simple endings: /t/, /d/, /ɪd/

a 🔊 **1.56** Listen and write the verbs in the table. Is the end of the verb pronounced /t/, /d/ or /ɪd/?

started   lived   played   wanted   ~~liked~~   decided
enjoyed   worked   danced   hated   loved
cooked   watched   visited   listened   talked

/t/	/d/	/ɪd/
liked		

8 Speak

Work with a partner or in a small group. Play a memory game. Use the verbs in the circle. How many verbs can you use in the past simple?

A: *Yesterday I listened to a CD.*
B: *Yesterday I listened to a CD and watched a film.*
C: *Yesterday I listened to a CD, watched a film and talked to a friend …*

cook   walk   play
decide   work   listen   dance
want   study
talk   start
learn   visit
watch

Describing someone

a 🔊 **1.59** Who is the person in the picture? Listen and check.

b 🔊 **1.59** Listen again and complete the conversation.

A: He ¹_____ _____ in London, England, in 1986. He's an ²_____ , ³_____ and a ⁴_____ . He's got ⁵_____ brown hair and ⁶_____ eyes. Who is it?

B: I don't know. Give ⁷_____ a clue.

A: OK. He ⁸_____ in *Harry Potter and the Goblet of Fire* and the *Twilight* films. Who is it?

c Work with a partner.

Student A: Turn to page 120.
Student B: Turn to page 122.

Portfolio 5

Biography of a famous person

a Look at the picture. What do you know about Bob Marley?

A **Robert Nesta Marley** was born on 6 February, 1945 in a small town in Jamaica. When he was ten, his father died and he moved with his mother to Kingston, the capital of Jamaica. The family didn't have very much money.

B When he was 14, Bob started to play music with his friends. Bob was the singer and songwriter and he also played the guitar. Bob and his band, The Wailers, played in Jamaica in the 1960s.

C In the 1970s, Bob Marley and The Wailers were international reggae stars. They travelled all over the world with their music. 'No woman, no cry', 'Three little birds' and 'One world, one love' were some of their songs. Many of Bob's songs were about peace or freedom.

D Bob died in Miami, USA in 1981, when he was 36. His last words were 'Money can't buy life'. After Bob died, millions of people continued to listen to and enjoy his music.

b Read the text and match the phrases with the paragraphs.

When/Where he died ....
Before he was famous ....
When/Where he was born ....
When he was famous ....

c Write a short biography (about 80 words) of a famous person from the past. Use some of the verbs in the box. Write about:

● when/where the person was born
● before the person was famous
● when the person was famous
● when/where the person died

be die have act live play like love
work study travel move want start visit

d Check your biography. Are the verbs in the past simple correct?

MAGICAL HISTORY TOUR
The Story of Liverpool

MERSEYSIDE MARITIME MUSEUM
28 July to 27 September
www.liverpoolmuseums.org.uk

FREE ENTRY

NATIONAL MUSEUMS LIVERPOOL

Liverpool | History

In 2007 it was Liverpool's 800th birthday. Liverpool began as a small fishing village but was the second city of the British Empire by the 19th century.

1207 – King John founded the city.

Early 1800s – 40% of the world's trade in sugar, cotton and tobacco passed through Liverpool.

Early 1900s – More immigrants came to Liverpool from Europe and Russia.

1700s – Liverpool became a very rich city. Unfortunately this was because Liverpool ships bought slaves in Africa and sold them in the USA and the Caribbean (until 1807). The beautiful buildings on the waterfront were built at this time.

1840s – Many Irish people came to the city because there was no food in Ireland. By 1851, 25% of the city was Irish.

1960s – Liverpool became world famous for music, especially the Beatles. Later, musicians like Echo and the Bunnymen, Frankie goes to Hollywood and Atomic Kitten also became famous.

TIMELINE

Mathew Street Music festival
Monday 27th August

MOUNTFORD HALL
University of Liverpool

Noon	Lady Madonna
1.15pm	U2UK
2.30pm	The Fillers
3.45pm	Antarctic Monkeys
5.00pm	Rollin Clones
6.00pm	Fleetwood Bac

KRAZY HOUSE
Wood Street

Noon	Oasisn't
1.15pm	Ded Hot Chilli Peppers

PRICE Free!

UEFA CHAMPIONS LEAGUE SEMI-FINAL
LIVERPOOL VERSUS CHELSEA
1ST LEG, ANFIELD   KICK-OFF 7.45PM

LIVERPOOL FC
Club Information

CLUB: Liverpool Football Club
INAUGURATION: 15 March 1892
CLUB COLOURS: Red & White
STADIUM ADDRESS: Anfield Road, Merseyside, Liverpool L4

TICKETS (Liverpool Home games)

TICKET PRICES:

Main stand and centenary stand	£34.00
Kop Grandstand	£32.00
Adult + Child:	£51.00

CITY GUIDE – LIVERPOOL

MAGICAL MYSTERY TOUR

Tours depart daily 2.30pm, from the 08 Place, Whitechapel

Advance booking recommended

T: 0151 236 9091 or 233 2459

bookings@liverpoolmagicalmysterytour.co.uk

No tours 25 and 26 December

www.caverncitytours.com

This two-hour long coach tour will introduce you to the lives of The Beatles, visiting their homes and schools as well as places that inspired some of their most memorable songs, such as 'Penny Lane' and 'Strawberry Fields Forever'.

An entertaining commentary tells the story as you travel around the city and its suburbs, finishing at the famous Cavern Club.

THE BEATLES STORY
LIVERPOOL

VISITOR INFORMATION

Opening Times
The Beatles Story is open 7 days a week, all year round (excluding 25/26 December). Opening hours are 9am–7pm. The last admission to the attraction is at 5pm.

Admission prices

Ticket type	Price	Conditions
Adult	£12.25	
Concession	£8.30	Students, Seniors & Unwaged. ID required.
Child	£6.35	Aged 5–16 years.
Under 5yrs	Free	
Family Saver 1	£36.25	2 adults and 3 children
Family Saver 2	£31.30	2 adults and 2 children

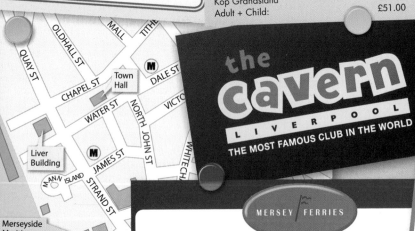

the Cavern
LIVERPOOL
THE MOST FAMOUS CLUB IN THE WORLD

MERSEY FERRIES

MONDAY – FRIDAY (River Explorer)

Pier Head [Depart]	Seacombe [Arrive/Depart]	Woodside [Arrive/Depart]	Pie[
10.00am	10.10am	10.20am	1
11.00am	11.10am	11.20am	
12.00pm			

---

1 Culture UK: Liverpool

a Look at the noticeboard about Liverpool and answer the questions.

1 Where can you see the Magical History Tour?
2 Which Liverpool club did The Beatles play in?
3 How many different places does the River Explorer go to?
4 How much is a ticket for the Mathew Street Music Festival?
5 What time does The Beatles Story open?
6 Was Liverpool a big city 800 years ago?
7 How much is a seat in the Kop Grandstand?
8 What time does the Magical Mystery Tour start?

b Complete the puzzle and find the mystery word.

1 A large area often used for football.
2 The colours of Liverpool FC. (3 words)
3 You go on these boats to cross water.
4 A person who visits a place.
5 The most famous night club in Liverpool.
6 The study of the past.

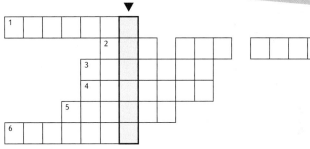

c Work with a partner. What would you like to do or see in Liverpool? Why?

2 Your project A timeline of a town

a Work in a group. Make a list of historic towns or cities in your country.

b Find out about one town or city from websites and books. Include information about:
- important events
- famous people

c Choose 5–7 important dates or periods of time and put them on a timeline.

d Draw a timeline for the town or city.

The Benito Juárez monument was built in 1967.

The Mexican President Benito Juárez was born in San Pablo Guelatao, Oaxaca, on the 21ˢᵗ March 1808. He studied law at Oaxaca Seminary and was the president of Mexico from 1867 to 1872.

In October 2006 there were protests in the streets of Oaxaca as teachers complained about the government.

The Aztecs became the dominating power in Oaxaca in the mid-1400s.

OAXACA, MEXICO

The Mixtecs and Zapotecs farmed, settled and expanded in the Oaxaca area for thousands of years.

On the 19ᵗʰ June 1821 General Antonio de León proclaimed the separation of the province of Oaxaca from the Spanish.

Oaxaca native Vinny Castilla had 320 home runs when he retired in 2007, the most of all Mexican Major League baseball players.

In August 1521 Hernan Cortez and the Spanish conquered the Aztecs. The Spanish started to rule Mexico as a colony.

Past simple: irregular verbs
Past simple: questions
Vocabulary: The natural world; Animals
Interaction 6: Taking turns

① **Geography lessons in Iceland**

② **Thousands of people can't fly to Iceland**

1 Read and listen

③ **Students escape when volcano erupts**

a Read the text quickly and choose the best title.

In April 2010, a group of 14 and 15-year-old students from Loughborough, in the UK, went to Iceland on a school trip. They wanted to see things they studied in their geography lessons at school

so they visited an area which has a lot of active volcanoes. However, in the middle of the night on Tuesday the 13th of April the Eyjafjallajökull volcano began to erupt.

Emergency services woke up the students and their teachers in their hotel at 4am. They didn't have time to get dressed and left in their pyjamas. A bus took them to Reykjavik, the capital of Iceland, where they were safe.

When Eyjafjallajökull erupted, it affected people all over the world. In the local area 800 people left their homes immediately because of floods from local rivers and dangerous smoke and gases. The volcano also sent a big cloud of

ash 8 km up into the air. This was dangerous for planes because the pilots couldn't see in the ash cloud.

Many countries in Europe, including the UK, France, Sweden and Norway, closed their airports for many days in April. Thousands of travellers around the world couldn't get home. They slept in airports or tried to get to their destinations by car, train, bus or even taxi!

Icelandic volcanoes are very active. When the volcano Laki erupted for eight months in 1783, almost two million people died around the world. It was the worst volcanic eruption in history. The students from Loughborough were lucky!

b 🔊 **2.1** Read the text again and listen. Are the sentences *right* (✓), *wrong* (✗) or *doesn't say* (−)?

1 The students learned about volcanoes before they went to Iceland.

2 They stayed near the Eyjafjallajökull volcano.

3 The volcano woke up the students.

4 The students enjoyed their trip to Iceland.

5 The eruption of Eyjafjallajökull didn't affect local people.

6 In April 2010 many airports closed in Europe.

7 Volcanoes in Iceland do not erupt very often.

8 The eruption of Laki in 1783 wasn't very big.

(2) Grammar Past simple: irregular verbs

a Look at the examples and complete the table.

> They didn't have time to get dressed.   A bus took them to Reykjavik

Positive	Negative
I/You/He/She/It/We/They	I/You/He/She/It/We/They .... **(did not) know**

Circle the correct words to complete the rules.

● The positive and the negative forms of the past simple are **the same / different** for all subjects.

● Irregular verbs **have / haven't** got the usual -ed ending in the past simple.

Grammar reference: Workbook page 90

b Find all the past simple verbs in the text in Exercise 1a. Which are regular? Which are irregular?

c Complete the sentences with the verbs in the past simple.

begin   not have   go   have   not know   not say   see   tell

1 John and Lisa .... to Bali on holiday last summer.

2 She .... hello to me this morning.

3 I .... the answers to the questions in my Maths exam.

4 We .... breakfast at 9 o'clock this morning.

5 He .... me about the party yesterday.

6 They're hungry because they .... breakfast.

7 The concert .... at 8 o'clock and finished two hours later.

8 We .... a good film at the cinema last weekend.

d Complete the story. Use the verbs in the past simple.

Yesterday I .... (get up) at .... (time). I .... (have) .... (food) for breakfast. I .... (go out) and I .... (meet) .... (famous person). He/She .... (say) .... (a sentence). We .... (go) to .... (a place) and we .... (see) a/an .... (one word).

e Now read your partner's story.

Check it out!

● We don't use *did* in positive sentences in the past simple.
I went to the cinema NOT ~~I did went to the cinema~~.

3 Vocabulary

The natural world

a 🔊 **2.2** Match the words with the pictures. Then listen and check.

> **1** beach **2** field **3** forest **4** hill
> **5** island **6** lake **7** mountain
> **8** river **9** sea **10** village

b Circle the correct words.

1 Britain is *a beach / an island*.
2 There's a new shop in the *village / lake*.
3 The Mediterranean and the Caribbean are *seas / rivers*.
4 We went on a boat on the *lake / field*.
5 The Andes in South America are *hills / mountains*.

c Which things in Exercise 3a are there near your town or city?

d Do you know any more things in the natural world? Write them down.

4 Speak

Work with a partner. Imagine you went on holiday to a place in one of the pictures in Exercise 3a. Tell your partner about your holiday. Use the verbs in the past simple.

> swim take go have eat see make
> play ride walk visit sleep come

····▷ *I went on holiday to the mountains.*
I swam in a lake and ate lots of fish.
We slept in a tent and made …

5 Vocabulary

Animals

a 🔊 **2.3** Match the words with the pictures. Then listen and check.

1 bear   2 bird
3 cow   4 dolphin
5 frog   6 monkey
7 mouse   8 penguin
9 spider   10 turtle

b 🔊 **2.4** Listen to six sounds. Which animals in Exercise 5a are they?

c Make word webs with the animals in Exercise 5a. Can you add more animals to the word webs?

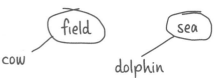

field — cow

sea — dolphin

forest — monkey

frog — lake

jungle — spider

6 Listen

a Look at the TV guide. What is *Amazing Animal Adventures* about?

1 animals in the circus ☐
2 animals in the jungle ☐
3 animals in the zoo ☐

b 🔊 **2.5** Listen to an interview with Anna, Jake, Sita and Marcus. Circle the animals they talk about.

birds dolphins frogs
monkeys snakes spiders

c 🔊 **2.5** Listen again and complete the sentences with the missing words.

1 Anna .... a door for the monkey house.
2 They .... the river dolphins.
3 They .... in the forest.
4 Jake .... a tarantula on his foot.
5 Sita .... a frog.
6 Marcus .... the jungle.

Amazing Animal Adventures
Wednesday 5.30pm–6 pm **BBC1**

This week Anna, Jake, Sita and Marcus help animals in the Amazon jungle and river.

Anna, 14, from Brighton

Jake, 14, from Belfast

Sita, 14, from Bradford

Marcus, 15, from Wiltshire

7 Grammar Past simple: questions

a Look at the examples and complete the table.

> ⤑ A: **Did** you **like** the jungle? B: *Yes, I* **did**.
>   A: *Where* **did** he **sleep**? B: *He* **slept** *in the forest.*

Yes/No questions

....................I/you/he/she/it/we/they	**like** the Amazon?

Short answers

Yes, I/You/He/She/It/We/They ....·
No, I/You/He/She/It/We/They ....**(did not)**.

Information questions

Where ....I/you/he/she/it/we/they **sleep**?

Answers

I/You/He/She/It/We/They ....in the forest.

(Circle) the correct word(s) to complete the rule.

● In past simple questions the verb forms are **the same** / **different** for all subjects (I/you/we/they/he/she/it), except for the verb **be** (was/were).

Grammar reference: Workbook page 90

Check it out!

Past time references

● Use *last* and *ago* to talk about the past.
  last *night/week/year/Saturday/June/summer*
  two hours/days/weeks/months **ago**

b 2.6 Put the words in the correct order. Then listen and check.

1 you / did / go / Where / last / weekend ?
....

2 Sunday / last / get up / you / When / did ?
....

3 TV / last / night / Did / watch / you ?
....

4 was / Who / your / last / year / English / teacher ?
....

5 your / friends / school / at / yesterday / Were ?
....

6 three / ago / hours / school / at / you / Were ?
....

c Work with a partner. Ask and answer the questions in Exercise 7b.

8 Pronunciation DVD

was: **strong and weak forms**

a 2.7 We can pronounce *was* /wəz/ or /wɒz/. Listen to the example.

> **Was** *the weather good? Yes, it* **was**.
> /wəz/   /wɒz/

b 2.8 Listen and (circle) the correct pronunciation of *was*.

1 /wəz/ /wɒz/   2 /wəz/ /wɒz/
3 /wəz/ /wɒz/   4 /wəz/ /wɒz/
5 /wəz/ /wɒz/   6 /wəz/ /wɒz/

c 2.9 Listen and repeat.

Where was William? Was he with you? No, he wasn't.

Interaction 6 DVD

Taking turns

a 2.10 Listen and tick (✓) the correct year.

2008 ☐   2010 ☐   2012 ☐

b 2.10 Listen again and put the sentences in the correct order.

A Can you repeat that, please? ☐
B I don't know how to say it. ☐
C OK. My turn. ☐
D Let's start. ☐
E Er, just a minute. ☐
F Can you spell that, please? ☐
G When did they go? ☐

c Work with a partner.
Student A: Turn to page 121.
Student B: Turn to page 123.

Portfolio 6

A travel diary

a Read Rebecca's travel diary. What animals did she see in Patagonia?

> <u>Tuesday, 9 July</u>
> Today Im in Ushuaia, a City in patagonia in Argentina.
>
> Patagonias a very big area in the south of argentina and Chile. There are beautiful mountains, lakes, forests and lots of animals. It's cold here because its winter at the moment!
>
> <u>thursday, 11 July</u>
> yesterday we went to a national park called Tierra del Fuego. We walked through a big forest near the mountains and we had lunch next to a river.
>
> <u>Friday, 12 july</u>
> This afternoon we went to the sea and saw sea elephants and penguins, but we didnt see any dolphins. It was great!

Sea elephants

b Read the diary again. Find and correct ten mistakes with punctuation and capital letters.

⤳ *Im = I'm*

c Write a travel diary (about 80 words) about a place you visited last year. Before you write, think about:

- the place you went to
- the things you saw (mountains, lakes, animals, etc.)
- the things you did

d Swap your travel diary with a partner. Check your partner's punctuation and capital letters.

Patagonia

Culture Vulture

Did you know that there are 14 national parks in Britain, for example Snowdonia and the Lake District? What national parks are there in your country?

Review ⑤ and ⑥

1 Grammar

a Circle the correct words.

1 Marilyn Monroe *was / were* a famous actress.
2 Pablo Picasso and Salvador Dalí *was / were* both Spanish artists.
3 Heath Ledger *wasn't / weren't* American but he lived in New York.
4 The Spice Girls *wasn't / weren't* called The Spice Girls in 1994. Their name was Touch.

☐ 4

b Complete the sentences with the verbs in the past simple.

> live   study   not play   enjoy   watch
> not like

1 They _____ Portuguese for five years at school.
2 I _____ coffee when I was a child, but I like it now.
3 We _____ a good programme on TV last night.
4 I _____ in France last year.
5 She _____ basketball yesterday.
6 I really _____ the concert last night. It was great!

☐ 6

c Complete the sentences with the verbs in the past simple.

1 We _____ (ride) our bicycles to the beach.
2 They _____ (go) on holiday to Greece in June.
3 I _____ (not eat) pizza every day when I was in Italy. There was a lot of different food.
4 Jack _____ (swim) a lot in the hotel pool.
5 We _____ (not know) that the sea was dangerous.
6 They _____ (take) a lot of photos of the mountains.
7 She _____ (see) a lot of tropical fish in the sea.
8 I _____ (not speak) much Spanish when I was in Mexico.

☐ 8

d Complete the questions with the verbs in the past simple.

> play   watch   get up   be born   go   see

1 _____ he _____ his new computer game yesterday?
2 _____ The Beatles _____ in London?
3 Where _____ your family _____ on holiday?
4 Who _____ you _____ yesterday?
5 _____ they _____ TV last night?
6 What time _____ you _____ last Saturday?

☐ 6

e Complete the biography of Elvis Presley. Choose the correct answer: A, B or C.

Elvis Presley, 'the king of Rock and Roll', ¹_____ the most popular singer of the 1950s. He was ²_____ in Mississippi in 1935, but later his parents ³_____ to Memphis and he ⁴_____ to school there. When he was nineteen he made his first record and soon he ⁵_____ famous all over the world. He ⁶_____ a lot of records – more than any other artist.

1	A is	B was	C were
2	A born	B lived	C borned
3	A lived	B stayed	C moved
4	A goes	B went	C was
5	A became	B become	C becomes
6	A sing	B made	C makes

☐ 6

How are you doing?

How many points have you got? Put two crosses on the chart: one for grammar and one for vocabulary.

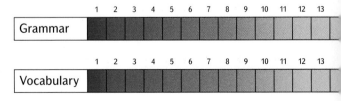

2 Vocabulary

a (Circle) the correct words.

1 She *is / has got* blue eyes.
2 He's *long / tall* and slim.
3 I've got *small / short* hair.
4 He *is / has* 20 years old.
5 They've got *long / tall* hair and brown eyes.
6 She had *blonde / grey* hair when she was a child.
7 She's got long *hair / hairs*.

|7|

b Complete the sentences with the words.

| model   photographer   actor   musician |
| dancer   writer   artist |

1 A .... uses a camera.
2 A .... plays or writes music.
3 An .... works in films.
4 A .... often appears in magazines.
5 An .... paints pictures.
6 A .... writes books.
7 A .... often works for a ballet company.

|7|

c Match the animals with the sentences.

| cow   monkey   frog   penguin   mouse |
| spider   dolphin |

1 It's very small and doesn't like cats.
....
2 It is small, usually green and lives in water.
....
3 It's a bird that lives in cold seas. ....
4 It lives in a field and gives milk. ....
5 It usually lives in trees. ....
6 It has got eight legs. ....
7 It's big and grey and lives in the sea.
....

|7|

d Complete the crossword. Use the clues to help you.

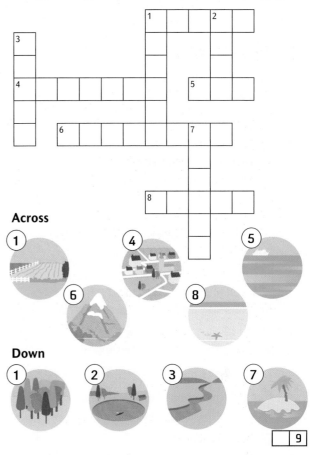

Across

①   ④   ⑤
⑥   ⑧

Down

①   ②   ③   ⑦

|9|

Correct it!

Correct these typical learner errors from Units 5 and 6.

1 It's got a big eyes and long hair.
....
2 The group only plaid for 35 minutes.
....
3 Last night there were a party on the beach.
....
4 I went and watch a film with her.
....
5 I swimmed in a lake.
....
6 Tony cames to my party.
....
7 I saw it about 6 month ago.
....
8 Do you liked the party last weekend?
....
9 She did went to the cinema.
....
10 It happened the last year, in the Olympics.
....

GREEN:	Great! Tell your teacher your score!
YELLOW:	Not bad, but go to the website for extra practice.
RED:	Talk to your teacher and look at Units 5 and 6 again. Go to the website for extra practice.

| 14 | 15 | 16 | 17 | 18 | 19 | 20 | 21 | 22 | 23 | 24 | 25 | 26 | 27 | 28 | 29 | 30 |

| 14 | 15 | 16 | 17 | 18 | 19 | 20 | 21 | 22 | 23 | 24 | 25 | 26 | 27 | 28 | 29 | 30 |

7 Mealtime

a/an, *some* and *any*
a lot of, *much* and *many*
Vocabulary: Food and drink; Food collocations
Interaction 7: Ordering food and drink

Sam Stern's
real food
"A great book..." Jamie Oliver
real fast

"a cracking book..." – Jamie Oliver
Sam Stern's
cooking up a storm
the teen survival cookbook

1 Read and listen

a Read the text and the recipes quickly. Then circle the topics in the text.

family   sport   food   school   pets   music   travel

Who is Sam Stern?

Sam Stern comes from Yorkshire in the north of England. He was born on the 29th of August 1990. He says he's got three fantastic sisters and a brilliant brother. One of his first memories is making bread with his mum. He learned everything he knows about cooking from her. Sam wrote his first cookbook when he was 14. It's for young people who enjoy cooking or who want to learn how to cook. It's got lots of simple recipes for teenagers. He thinks it's important for young people to eat good food. 'Purple, red and orange fruit and vegetables are great,' he says.

Sam always listens to music when he writes his cookbooks. He says it helps him write. He often listens to Razorlight, Franz Ferdinand and the Red Hot Chili Peppers.

He loves music and he would like to learn to play the guitar. He wants to go to China because he loves Chinese food.

b 🔊 2.12 Read the text again and listen. Then answer the questions.

1 What are the titles of Sam's first two books?
2 How many children are there in Sam's family?
3 Who taught Sam to cook?
4 What food does Sam think is great?
5 When does Sam listen to music?
6 Does Sam play the guitar?
7 Where does Sam want to go?
8 What do you need to make Sam's pizza bread?

c Work with a partner. Do you know any quick recipes like Sam's? Tell your partner.

Sam's quick recipes

Banana and orange smoothie
Mix some orange juice, a banana, some milk, yoghurt and honey. Put it in a glass and drink.

Pizza bread
Put some oil, tomato sauce and cheese on some bread and cook for five minutes.

2 ⟩ Vocabulary

Food and drink

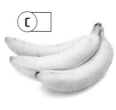

a 🔊 **2.13** Match the words with the pictures.
Then listen and check.

| 1 apple juice 2 bananas 3 biscuits 4 carrots |
| 5 grapes 6 ham 7 lemonade 8 milk 9 onions |
| 10 pasta 11 potatoes 12 salad 13 steak |
| 14 strawberries 15 tuna |

b Complete the table with the words in Exercise 2a.

Fruit	Vegetables	Meat and fish	Drinks	Other food
....	....	....	....	....
....	....	....	....	....
....	....	....	....	....

c What food or drink in Exercise 2a do you have
every day/week? What do you never eat/drink?

3 ⟩ Grammar

a/an, some and any

a Look at the examples and complete the table.

> ⤑ *I've got **an orange** and **a banana** for lunch.*
> *They always have **eggs** for breakfast.*
> *We had **rice** and **chicken** last night.*

Countable nouns	Uncountable nouns
an orange	rice
a	....
....	

(Circle) the correct word to complete the rule.

● We use *a* or *an* with singular **countable** /
uncountable nouns.

Grammar reference: Workbook page 92

b Write *C* (countable nouns) or *U* (uncountable nouns).

cheese ....   bread ....
book ....   money ....
water ....   house ....
sandwich ....   computer ....

Check it out!

some and **any**

● Use *some* and *any* with plural nouns
and uncountable nouns.
● Use *some* in positive sentences.
● Use *any* in negative sentences and in
questions.

c (Circle) the correct words.

1 We need *some* / *any* onions from
the supermarket.
2 There aren't *an* / *any* CDs in my bag.
3 Is there *a* / *any* dog in the garden?
4 There are *some* / *any* magazines on the table.
5 Would you like *a* / *an* orange?
6 There isn't *some* / *any* ham in my sandwich.
7 We've got *some* / *any* homework.
8 There are *any* / *some* biscuits.

4 Grammar

a lot of, much and many

a 🔊 **2.14** Ginny and Steve want to make a pizza. Listen and tick (✓) the food you hear.

bread	*cheese*
ham	*onions*
olives	*chicken*
oil	*tomato sauce*

b Look at the examples and complete the table.

> *There are **a lot of** apples. There's **a lot of** cheese.*
> *There are**n't many** olives. There is**n't much** tomato sauce.*

Countable nouns		**Uncountable nouns**	
There are	oranges.	There's	rice.
There are**n't**		There is**n't**	
How **many** apples are there?		How **much** cheese is there?	

(Circle) the correct words to complete the rules.

- We normally use *a lot of* in **positive** / **negative** sentences.
- We use *much* and *many* in **positive** / **negative** sentences and questions.

Grammar reference: Workbook page 92

c 🔊 **2.15** (Circle) the correct words. Listen and check.

1 How *much / many* cheese is there?
2 There's not *much / many* ham.
3 How *much / many* olives are there?
4 There are *a lot of / many* onions.
5 There aren't *many / much* oranges.

d Make questions with *How much* or *How many*.

1 water / drink every day?

....

2 students / in your class?

....

3 hours / sleep every night?

....

4 money / have in your bag or pocket?

....

5 subjects / study at school?

....

e Work with a partner. Ask and answer the questions in Exercise 4d.

5 Pronunciation 📀

/e/ and /æ/

a 🔊 **2.16** Listen to the /e/ and /æ/ sounds in these words.

/e/	p**e**n	h**ea**d
/æ/	m**a**n	h**a**ve

b 🔊 **2.17** Listen and tick (✓) the correct column.

	/e/	/æ/
any		
apple		
bread		
carrot		
egg		
ham		
lemon		
many		
pasta		
pepper		
sandwich		
salad		

c 🔊 **2.18** Listen and check.

d 🔊 **2.19** Listen and repeat.

> *There's an egg and an apple and a carrot on my head.*

6 Speak

Work with a partner. Student A: Look at the picture of the fridge for one minute, then close your book. Student B: Ask questions about the picture of the fridge. How much can Student A remember? Then change roles.

B: *Is there any milk?*
A: *Yes, I think so.*
B: *Correct! How many apples are there?*
A: *There aren't any apples ....*

7 Vocabulary

Food collocations

a Look at the menu. <u>Underline</u> the correct options.

b Circle the correct words.

1 I'd like *an apple* / *a veggie* burger, please.
2 Would you like a *tomato* / *milk* salad?
3 Is there a *cheese* / *pasta* sandwich?
4 They've got some *vanilla* / *onion* ice cream.
5 There's some *strawberry* / *carrot* soup.
6 We need some *orange* / *potato* juice.
7 Can I have a *chocolate* / *ham* milkshake?

c Work with a partner. Match the words to make more food and drink collocations.

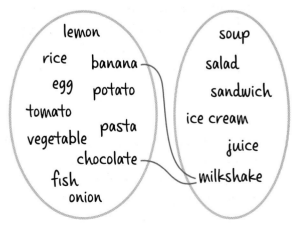

(8) Listen

a 🔊 **2.20** Listen to two conversations. Where are the people?

at home ☐   in a café ☐   in a supermarket ☐

b 🔊 **2.20** Listen again and tick (✓) the correct answer: A, B or C.

1 What does the boy have to eat?

A ☐    B ☐ 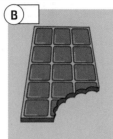   C ☐

2 What does he have to drink?

A ☐    B ☐ 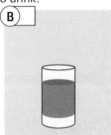   C ☐

3 What does the girl have to eat?

A ☐    B ☐    C ☐

4 What does she have to drink?

A ☐    B ☐    C ☐

5 How much is the girl's food and drink?

A ☐    B ☐    C ☐

Interaction 7 (DVD)

Ordering food and drink

a 🔊 **2.21** Listen and put the sentences in the correct order.

Sorry, we haven't got any lemonade. .... ☐

Can I help you? .... ☐

That's £2.70, please. .... ☐

Can I have a lemonade? .... ☐

Yes, here you are. Anything else? .... ☐

Can I have a cheese and ham sandwich? .... ☐

OK. Umm, an orange juice, please. .... ☐

b 🔊 **2.21** Listen again and write W (waiter) or C (customer) next to each sentence.

c Work with a partner.

Student A and B: Turn to page 124.

Portfolio 7

A recipe

a Read the text. What food is in a traditional English breakfast?

An English Breakfast Sandwich

The English breakfast is famous all over the world. People usually have it when they are on holiday or at the weekend because it's a very big breakfast. When people have an English breakfast they always have bacon and eggs and they sometimes have other things like tomatoes, sausages and beans.

Here is a recipe for an English breakfast sandwich.

Ingredients	Instructions
bread (2 pieces) a tomato bacon an egg some oil salt and pepper	**1** Toast the bread. **2** Slice the tomato. **3** Fry the tomato, bacon and egg in some oil. **4** Put one piece of toast on a plate. Add the bacon, then the egg, then the tomato. Add some salt and pepper. Put the other piece of toast on top.

Your sandwich is ready to eat. Enjoy it!

b Read the instructions in the recipe again and put the pictures in the correct order.

c Circle the imperatives in the instructions.

⸺▷ Toast the bread.

d Write a recipe for a new sandwich.
Before you write, think about:

- the name
- the ingredients
- the instructions

Culture Vulture

Did you know that most people in Britain (over 60%) have cereal or toast for breakfast? What do people have for breakfast in your country?

From bush food to barbecues

Australia is a huge country and it has a lot of different kinds of food. In the past, the Aboriginal people of Australia ate animals like crocodiles and some insects like the witchetty grub. Aboriginal Australians travelled around the Australian countryside, or 'bush', to find food.

When the first British and Irish people moved to Australia in the 1830s, they brought sheep and cows from Europe. They also brought traditional English and Irish recipes. Many of these recipes, like fish and chips and meat pies, are still popular today. They also created new Australian recipes such as the *pavlova* (a fruit dessert) and *damper* (a bread cooked in the bush).

After 1945, a lot more people came to live in Australia from countries like Italy, Germany, Greece, Thailand and India. They brought recipes with them and Australians began to eat and drink different things. People started to drink espresso coffee and eat Mediterranean and Asian food.

A lot of modern Australians love cooking with fresh food. They often cook food on barbecues in their gardens or on the beach. Today more people also eat Aboriginal food like kangaroo and emu. Mark Olive, an Aboriginal chef, has a popular television cookery programme about traditional bush food. There are always new recipes to try in Australia!

The witchetty grub. Mmm, delicious!

The pavlova, named after a Russian dancer.

Mark Olive, an Aboriginal TV chef.

Kangaroo or emu for lunch?

Meat pies are popular.

1 ▸ Culture World: Australia

a What do you know about Australian food? Do the quiz before you read the magazine page. (Circle) the correct answers.

Australia Quiz

1 Which three animals live in Australia?

  A crocodile   **B** lion
  C kangaroo   **D** emu

2 Who were the first Europeans to live in Australia?

  A Germans   **B** Spanish
  C Greeks and Italians
  D British and Irish

3 Which three types of food are popular in Australia?

  A Asian   **B** Mediterranean
  C African   **D** bush food

b Now read the magazine page quickly and check your answers.

c Read the magazine page again. Are the sentences *right* (✓), *wrong* (✗) or *doesn't say* (–)?

1 Australia does not have many different types of food. ☐

2 In the past, Aboriginal people found food in different places. ☐

3 British and Irish people brought food and recipes to Australia. ☐

4 The people who arrived after 1945 didn't like Australian food. ☐

5 Australians like food from countries like Italy, Greece and Thailand. ☐

6 Cooking outside is popular in Australia. ☐

7 Today many people in Australia eat crocodile. ☐

d Find words in the magazine page that mean …

1 very big (paragraph 1) ....

2 a name for the first people in Australia (paragraph 1)

....

3 somewhere to cook food outside (paragraph 4)

....

e Which Australian food would/wouldn't you like to eat? Why?/Why not?

2 ▸ Your project

Traditional and modern food

a Work in a group. Make two lists of food from your country: traditional and modern.

b Make a poster. Write a short description of each type of food.

TRADITIONAL

Torun in Poland is famous for gingerbread.

Gingerbread is a type of biscuit. It's my favourite food!

Pierogi ★

Delicious!

Wild blueberries

MODERN

Potato dumplings and sour cream!

Chłodnik

Pizza is popular. I love it! ★

Cold beetroot soup.

8 At home

Comparative adjectives
Superlative adjectives
Vocabulary: Parts of a house; Furniture and objects
Interaction 8: Describing a room

1 Vocabulary

Parts of a house

a 🔊 **2.22** Match the words with the letters in the picture. Then listen and check.

1 bathroom **2** bedroom **3** dining room
4 garden **5** hall **6** kitchen
7 living room **8** stairs

b Make questions and then write true answers.

1 Where / you / eat / dinner ?

....

2 Where / you / listen / music ?

....

3 Where / you / use / computer ?

....

4 Where / you / have / shower ?

....

5 Where / you / read / books ?

....

c Work with a partner. Ask and answer the questions in Exercise 1b.

Culture Vulture

Did you know that 80% of people in Britain live in houses? Do people in your country live in houses or flats?

② Read and listen

a Read the texts quickly and match them with pictures A and B.

Modern or traditional?

1 ☐

The Mishra family live in Delhi, the capital of India. Shristi, a 15-year-old girl, and Sarvocch, a 14-year-old boy, live with ¹ .... father, Nagendra, and their mother, Anita. Every day they travel 20km into the city centre to study and to work. They live in a modern flat with two bedrooms, a small kitchen and ² .... living room. They usually eat in one of the bedrooms, sitting ³ .... the floor. The family often watch TV together in the living room.

Nagendra lived in a village when he ⁴ .... young, but he and all his friends moved to the city to work. He enjoyed living in the countryside but he says that life in the city is more comfortable.

2 ☐

Three generations of the Gupta family live in this traditional Indian house called a *bhunga*: a grandfather, the parents and four children. The house is very pretty. There ⁵ .... small mirrors on the inside walls and the women paint the outside walls every year during the Indian festival of Diwali.

When there was a big earthquake in western India, ⁶ .... modern houses fell down. The traditional houses did not because they are round and very strong. In summer, when the temperature is 46° outside, the *bhungas* are cool because the walls are very thick. In the houses there ⁷ .... traditional beds with long legs and there aren't ⁸ .... tables or chairs.

b 🔊 2.23 Read the texts again and choose the correct answer: A, B or C. Then listen and check.

1 A they	**B** their	**C** the	
2 A an	**B** a	**C** some	
3 A in	**B** next to	**C** on	
4 A was	**B** were	**C** is	

5 A is	**B** has	**C** are	
6 A much	**B** a lot of	**C** any	
7 A are	**B** is	**C** have	
8 A any	**B** much	**C** a lot of	

③ Grammar

Comparative adjectives

a Look at the examples and complete the table.

⟶ *The traditional house is **stronger**
than the flat.
The traditional house is **prettier than**
the flat.
Life in the city is **more comfortable**
than the country.*

Adjective	Comparative	
strong	....	
small	**smaller**	
big	**bigger**	
pretty	....	(than) …
sunny	**sunnier**	
comfortable	....	
beautiful	**more beautiful**	

	Irregular comparative	
good	**better**	
bad	**worse**	(than) …
far	**further**	

(Circle) the correct words to complete
the rules.

- For adjectives of **one syllable /
two or more syllables**, make
the comparative by adding *-er*.
- If an adjective ends in *-y*, make the
comparative by changing the *-y* to **-er/-ier**.
- For adjectives of **one syllable /
two or more syllables**, the comparative
is *more* + adjective.

Grammar reference: Workbook page 94

---

b Complete the sentences. Use the comparative
form of the adjectives.

1 A tortoise is .... (slow) than
a horse.

2 A bike is .... (expensive)
than a skateboard.

3 Maths homework is ....
(boring) than playing computer games.

4 A dolphin is .... (big) than
a monkey.

5 Robert is .... (tall) than
Michael.

6 Spain is .... (sunny)
than Scotland.

7 Bridget is .... (strong)
than her little sister.

④ Vocabulary

Furniture and objects

a 🔊 2.24 Match the words with the pictures.
Then listen and check.

1 bath	**2** bed	**3** cooker	**4** cupboard	**5** desk
6 fridge	**7** rug	**8** shower	**9** sofa	**10** wardrobe

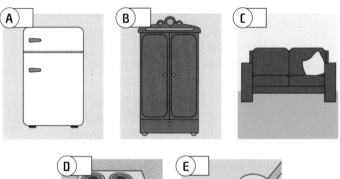

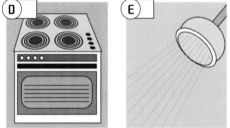

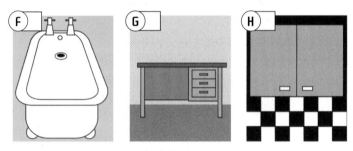

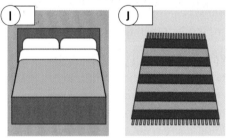

b Complete the table with the words in Exercise 4a.
Do you know any more words? Write them down.

bathroom	bedroom	kitchen	living room

c What furniture and objects do you have in your
bedroom?

5 Listen

a 🔊 2.25 Look at the pictures 1–4. Can you match the houses with the people? Listen and check.

A
Salvador Dalí

B
Martin Luther King

C
Marie Curie

D
Victoria Beckham

b 🔊 2.25 Listen again. Are the sentences *right* (✓) or *wrong* (✗)? Correct the wrong sentences.

1 Victoria Beckham's house is cheap.
2 The rooms in the first house are big.
3 Martin Luther King's house is small.
4 Salvador Dalí's house is modern.
5 Marie Curie's house isn't traditional.
6 People are living in the fourth house now.

c Work with a partner. Which is your favourite house? Why?

6 Pronunciation 🔵DVD

The schwa /ə/ in comparatives

a 🔊 2.26 Listen to the /ə/ sound in these words.

Houses are bigger than flats.
     /ə/   /ə/

b 🔊 2.27 Listen and (circle) the /ə/ sounds in the comparative forms.

1 The countryside is **cheaper than** the city.
2 A chair is **smaller than** a sofa.
3 Cars are **faster than** bicycles.
4 Winter is **colder than** autumn.

c 🔊 2.28 Listen and repeat.

I'm bigger than you, and stronger than you, and faster than you, and better than you!

7 Speak

Work with a partner. Compare a city and a village in your country. Use the adjectives.

slow happy bad
comfortable cheap beautiful
fast boring interesting
good expensive

····> *I think people are happier in ...*
     I think life is better in ...

8 Grammar

Superlative adjectives

a Match the pictures with the texts.

A The world's heaviest rabbit

At 18 months old it weighs nearly 13 kilos!

B The world's most expensive piano

John Lennon bought this in 1970 and in 2000 George Michael bought it for $2.1 million.

C The tallest chair in Italy

It's 20m high and weighs 22,910kg.

D The world's fastest sofa

In 2007 Marek Turowski drove this at 148kph in Leicestershire, England.

b Look at the examples in Exercise 8a and complete the table.

Adjective	Superlative	
long		longest
fast		....
pretty	**the**	prettiest
heavy		....
expensive		....
beautiful		most beautiful

	Irregular superlative	
good		best
bad	**the**	worst
far		furthest

Circle the correct words to complete the rules.

- For adjectives of **one syllable / two or more syllables**, make the superlative by adding -est.
- If an adjective ends in -y, make the superlative by changing the -y to -iest.
- For adjectives of **one syllable / two or more syllables**, the superlative is *the most* + adjective.

Grammar reference: Workbook page 94

Check it out!

- We don't use *the* with comparative adjectives.
  He's better than me at Maths.
  NOT
  ~~He's the better than me at Maths.~~

c Complete the sentences. Use the superlative form of the adjectives.

big expensive heavy long

1 .... skateboard in 2005 was 9.17m long.
2 .... mobile is 2.05m x 0.83m x 0.45m.
3 .... tiramisu in 2007 weighed 305.95kg.
4 .... jeans in 2005 cost $60,000.

d Write six questions.

Who What Where	is the	biggest smallest most difficult happiest most boring most interesting	subject room singer sport object person	in your house? on TV? at school? in your country? in the world?

e Work with a partner. Ask and answer the questions in Exercise 8d.

Interaction 8

Describing a room

a 🔊 **2.29** Listen and tick (✓) the correct picture.

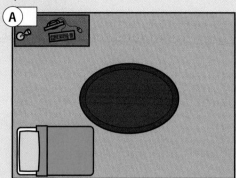

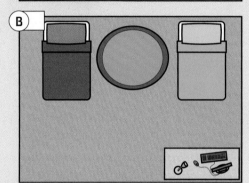

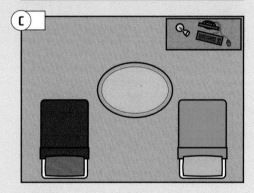

b 🔊 **2.30** Complete the diagram with the phrases. Then listen and check.

> at the bottom   at the top   in the middle
> on the left   on the right

1 ....

2 .... 3 .... 4 ....

5 ....

c Work with a partner.

Student A: Turn to page 121.
Student B: Turn to page 123.

Portfolio 8

My dream room

a Read about Adam's dream room. Name three things he has got in his room.

b Eight different words in the text are wrongly spelled. Can you correct them?

> This is a picture of my dream room. It's the bigest and best room in the hous. It's bigger than my brother's room!
>
> There's a huge, confortable bed in the middle of the room but that's not my favourit thing. I love my TV. It's fantastic. I can watch all my films and play video games on it.
>
> My computor is on a desk near the bed. It's really mordern — better than all my friends' computors. There's an electric gitar and a drum kit. I'm in a band and we practise in my big room.
>
> There are really big windoes and a balcony. I can see the sea from the balcony. I love this room. It's amazing!

c Write a description of your dream room. Before you write, think about:

- the furniture in the room
- the position of the furniture in the room
- your favourite thing in the room

d Check your description for spelling mistakes.

OUR HOUSE

1 Song

a Choose six of these words and write them in the bingo card.

> house   downstairs   father   gets up
> street   playing   mother   work   school
> Sunday   sister   brother

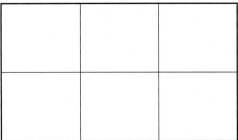

b 🔊 **2.31** Listen to the song and cross out the words when you hear them. Say 'Bingo!' when you cross out all the words.

c 🔊 **2.32** Listen and put the pictures in the correct order. Write the numbers in the boxes.

d 🔊 **2.33** Listen to part of the song again and ⊙circle the correct words.

Our house, it *has / doesn't have* a crowd
There's *usually / always* something happening
And it's usually quite *loud / quiet*.
Our *mum / sister*, she's so houseproud
No one / Nothing ever slows her down
And a mess is not allowed

Our house, in the middle of our street
Our house, in the middle of our
Our house, in the middle of our street
Our house, in the middle of our

Father gets up *early / late* for work
Mother has to iron his *shirt / trousers*
Then she sends the kids to *school / work*
Sees them off with a *small / big* kiss
She's the one they're going to miss
In lots of ways.

e Would you like to live in 'Our house'? Why? / Why not?

sister

father

mother

brother

the kids

2 Sound check

a 🔊 2.34 Listen to four sentences and count the syllables.

1 ☐ 2 ☐ 3 ☐ 4 ☐

b 🔊 2.34 Listen again and write the sentences.

c 🔊 2.34 Listen again and repeat.

3 Musical notes

The song *Our House* is by a British group called Madness. They were popular in Britain in the 1980s. People started to use computers in music and created styles such as house music and techno. There were also very unusual styles of fashion at this time. Punks wore clothes that sometimes frightened the older generations.

Madness

House music

Punks

a 🔊 2.35 Listen to the extracts. What do you think the music is like? Write the adjectives next to the types of music.

noisy	happy	fun	repetitive	electronic	angry	bad	boring	good

1 Punk   ....
2 Ska   ....
3 House music ....
4 Disco   ....

b Now use the adjectives to make comparative sentences about the types of music in Exercise 3a.

Review 7 and 8

1 Grammar

a Complete the sentences. Use *a*, *an*, *some* or *any*.

1 I'd like .... oranges and bananas, please.
2 Can I have .... pen, please?
3 There isn't .... milk in the fridge.
4 I haven't got .... money.
5 Do you want .... apple?
6 There aren't .... people on the bus.

[6]

b Circle the correct words.

1 How *much / many* water is there?
2 There isn't *much / many* bread.
3 How *much / many* books have you got?
4 There aren't *much / many* students at school today.
5 How *much / many* rice would you like?
6 There are *many / a lot of* pictures in the book.
7 They haven't got *much / many* friends.

[7]

c Complete the table with the comparative and superlative forms of the adjectives.

Adjective	Comparative	Superlative
slow		
hot		
happy		
beautiful		
good		
bad		

[6]

d Use the words to make comparative and superlative sentences.

1 frog   elephant   cat   (small)

....

....

2 car   bicycle   plane   (fast)

....

....

3 town   village   country   (big)

....

....

4 father   son   grandfather   (old)

....

....

5 bear   monkey   mouse   (dangerous)

....

....

[5]

e Read the article about Briony. Choose the correct answer: A, B or C.

> Briony lives in Canada and she loves cooking. She can make ¹ .... different things, but her favourite recipe is for chocolate cake. She thinks that her cakes are ² .... than the cakes you buy from a shop. She's doing ³ .... cooking classes at the college near her house and there's ⁴ .... cooking club at her school. When Briony and her friends cook something at school, they see how ⁵ .... the same thing is at the supermarket. Usually it is ⁶ .... when they make it.

1 **A** any   **B** a lot of   **C** much
2 **A** the best   **B** good   **C** better
3 **A** some   **B** a   **C** any
4 **A** a   **B** an   **C** some
5 **A** many   **B** much   **C** are
6 **A** more cheap   **B** cheapest   **C** cheaper

[6]

How are you doing?

How many points have you got? Put two crosses on the chart: one for grammar and one for vocabulary.

	1	2	3	4	5	6	7	8	9	10	11	12	13
Grammar													

	1	2	3	4	5	6	7	8	9	10	11	12	13
Vocabulary													

2 Vocabulary

a Put the letters in the correct order and make eight food and drink words.

1 nanaba ....
2 otcarr ....
3 ttighespa ....
4 awrrbeiesstr ....
5 ionson ....
6 eirc ....
7 utan ....
8 lkim ....

| | 8 |

b Match the foods (1–7) with (A–G).

1 banana   **A** oil
2 orange   **B** soup
3 tomato   **C** juice
4 vanilla   **D** smoothie
5 cheese   **E** salad
6 tuna   **F** ice cream
7 olive   **G** burger

| | 7 |

c Complete the sentences with the words.

bathroom bedroom dining room
garden living room kitchen hall

1 We often sit on the sofa and watch TV in the ....
2 I cook in the ....
3 My two sisters sleep in a big ....
4 They have dinner in the ....
5 We keep our coats in the ....
6 There's a big apple tree in our ....
7 My brother is having a shower in the ....

| | 7 |

d Complete the puzzle and find the mystery word.

1 You stand up and wash in this.
2 You sit down and wash in this.
3 You put food in this. It's cold.
4 You sleep in this.
5 You put this on the floor.
6 You sit on this. It's comfortable.
7 You put things in this. It usually has shelves.
8 You do your homework on this.

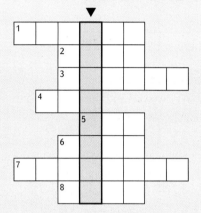

| | 8 |

Correct it!

Correct these typical learner errors from Units 7 and 8.

1 There are a lot of differents animals.

....

2 How much are this things?

....

3 I want to buy some cheese, a bread and some tomatoes.

....

4 I haven't got CDs.

....

5 I want to buy some fruits for my friend.

....

6 I think the bester place to go is the beach.

....

7 I was the baddest boy in my class.

....

8 I think it is the more interesting place in my town.

....

9 I like this room because is bigger.

....

10 I like Italian food very much. The beast is spaghetti.

....

GREEN: Great! Tell your teacher your score!
YELLOW: Not bad, but go to the website for extra practice.
RED: Talk to your teacher and look at Units 7 and 8 again. Go to the website for extra practice.

| 14 | 15 | 16 | 17 | 18 | 19 | 20 | 21 | 22 | 23 | 24 | 25 | 26 | 27 | 28 | 29 | 30 |

| 14 | 15 | 16 | 17 | 18 | 19 | 20 | 21 | 22 | 23 | 24 | 25 | 26 | 27 | 28 | 29 | 30 |

9 Go to town

Present continuous for future plans
Prepositions of place
Vocabulary: Buildings and places; Shops
Interaction 9: Asking for and giving directions

1 Read and listen

a Read the texts quickly and match them with the pictures.

We stopped some British teenagers in the street and asked them ...

'What are you doing this weekend?'

1 ☐ **Max, nearly 16!** It's my 16th birthday tomorrow so my mum and dad are taking me, my sister and some friends paintballing. It's really fun. You have two teams and the idea is to shoot everyone in the other team with paintballs. I can't wait! On Sunday I'm not doing anything special – only watching TV.

2 ☐ **Abigail, 16** Tomorrow afternoon I'm going shopping. I'm meeting some friends at a café in the shopping centre. On Sundays I play the violin in an orchestra. We're giving a concert next week.

3 ☐ **Saira, 15** I've got a big school project to do this weekend. On Saturday morning I'm meeting some friends at the library in town. There are a lot of good books and the internet is free. Then, the day after tomorrow I'm going 'bouldering' at the sports centre. They've got a special 'bouldering' wall that we can climb.

4 ☐ **Ethan, 15** Our Scout group meet every Saturday and tomorrow we're helping at the local hospital. I really enjoy meeting new people. On Sunday I'm going to the cinema with some friends.

5 ☐ **Keiran, 14** This Sunday my brother and I are racing in a mountain bike competition. He's much better than me – and he can do really amazing jumps. Our parents and some of our friends are coming to watch us so I hope I do well. On Saturday I'm going swimming – I go every Saturday.

→ Next month: The best towns in Britain.   ✉ Send us an email and tell us why your town is the best in Britain.

b 🔊 2.36 Read the texts again and listen. Then complete the table with the activities for each person.

	Saturday	Sunday
Max		
Abigail		
Saira		
Ethan		
Keiran		

c Who do you think has the most interesting weekend plans? Why?

Culture Vulture

Did you know that there are about 400,000 Scouts in the UK and about 28 million Scouts in different countries around the world? Are there Scouts in your country?

② Grammar

Present continuous for future plans

a Look at the examples and complete the table.

> Tomorrow lunchtime we**'re helping** at the local hospital.
> On Sunday I**'m not doing** anything special.
> What **are** you **doing** this weekend?

Positive

I	.... **(am)**			
He/She/It	.... **(is)**	do**ing**		
You/We/They	.... **(are)**	help**ing**		

Negative

I	'm not **(am not)**		
He/She/It	.... **(is not)**	do**ing**	
You/We/They	aren't **(are not)**	help**ing**	

Yes/No questions

Am	I		
Is	he/she/it	help**ing**?	
....	you/we/they		

Short answers

Yes, I	No, I**'m not**.
Yes, he/she/it **is**.	No, he/she/it **isn't**.
Yes, you/we/they **are**.	No, you/we/they **aren't**.

Ⓒircle the correct word to complete the rule.

● We use the present continuous to talk about **past** / **future** arrangements.
(Remember – we also use the present continuous to talk about the present!)

Grammar reference: Workbook page 86

b Complete the sentences with the verbs in the present continuous.

not do   go   not go out   have   play   watch

1 I .... volleyball for the school team next Wednesday.
2 She .... shopping with her friends tomorrow.
3 He .... with his friends this weekend, he's staying at home.
4 .... you .... the football match on TV tonight?
5 I .... my homework tonight because I'm going to the cinema.
6 .... they .... a party next Friday?

c Put the words in the correct order.

1 playing / tomorrow / I'm / hockey

....

2 this / He's / weekend / going / cinema / to / the

....

3 having / They're / grandmother / lunch / next / with / Sunday / their

....

4 are / What / doing / weekend / next / you ?

....

d Work with a partner. Ask and answer questions about your future plans.

What are you doing …

1 tonight?   4 this weekend?
2 tomorrow evening?   5 on Sunday morning?
3 the day after tomorrow?   6 next week?

> I'm playing basketball tonight.

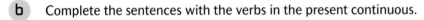

③ Vocabulary Buildings and places

a 🔊 **2.37** Match the words with the numbers in the picture. Then listen and check.

☐ bank ☐ café ☐ car park ☐ football ground ☐ library
☐ museum ☐ post office ☐ shopping centre ☐ station

b Make word webs with the places in Exercise 3a.

go to a concert
football ground
play football
watch a match

c What other buildings and places can you see in the picture? Write them down.

d Which places in Exercise 3a are there where you live?

4 Listen

a 🔊 **2.38** Listen and find Zach, Diana and Sally on the map in Exercise 3a. Write the correct letter next to each name.

Zach ....   Diana ....   Sally ....

b 🔊 **2.38** Listen again and match the people with the activities and the times.

Zach	is	watching a football match	at	7:00pm
Diana		going to the cinema		7:15pm
Sally		going for a pizza		7:30pm
		playing football		7:45pm
		playing volleyball		8:00pm

5 Grammar

Prepositions of place

a Look at the diagrams, the map in Exercise 3a and the example. Complete the sentences with the correct prepositions.

┈┈➤ *Zach is in front of the sports centre.*

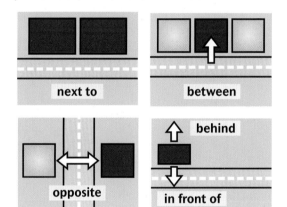

next to   between   opposite   behind   in front of

1 Diana is at the café .... the school and the football ground.
2 Sally is at the café .... the cinema.
3 The boy in the red T-shirt is at the shopping centre .... the café.
4 The boy in the orange T-shirt is in the park .... the school.
5 The girl in the blue T-shirt is .... the football ground.

Grammar reference: Workbook page 94

b 🔊 **2.39** Write sentences about the picture in Exercise 3a. Use the prepositions in Exercise 5a. Then listen and check.

1 postman / post office
   The postman is behind the post office.
2 bank / library
   ....
3 car park / supermarket / sports centre
   ....
4 hotel / shopping centre
   ....
5 station / museum
   ....

Check it out!

Multiple-word prepositions
● Some prepositions of place have more than one word.
   *in front **of***
   *next **to***

6 Pronunciation 📀

Linking words

a 🔊 **2.40** Listen to how these words link together.

Tom's⌣in
front⌣of the cinema
Tom's⌣in front⌣of the cinema

b 🔊 **2.41** Listen to the sentences and draw a line between the words that are linked. Then listen again and repeat.

1 The bank's opposite the cinema.
2 There are three people in the café.
3 The buses are in front of the museum.
4 There's a post office in the shopping centre.

c 🔊 **2.42** Listen and repeat.

*Charlotte and Beth are in the post office
in front of the hotel and café.*

(7) Speak

Work with a partner. Student A: Look at the picture in Exercise 3a on page 80 for one minute, then close your book. Student B: Ask questions about the people and places in the picture. How much can Student A remember? Then change roles.

B: *Where's Zach?*
A: *He's opposite the cinema.*
B: *No, he isn't.*
A: *Is he in front of the sports centre?*

(8) Vocabulary

Shops

a 🔊 **2.43** Match the words with the pictures of the things you can buy at the shops. Then listen and check.

> 1 bookshop   2 chemist's
> 3 clothes shop   4 newsagent's
> 5 pet shop   6 shoe shop
> 7 supermarket   8 travel agent's

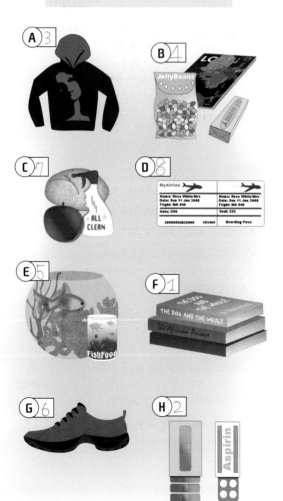

A) 3
B) 4
C) 7
D) 8
E) 5
F) 1
G) 6
H) 2

---

b 🔊 **2.44** Listen to the people. Where are they? Write the shops.

1 ....   4 ....
2 ....   5 ....
3 ....   6 ....

c Do you know any other things you can buy in the shops? Make word webs.

Interaction 9 DVD

Asking for and giving directions

a 🔊 **2.45** Listen to the directions. Choose the correct map: 1, 2 or 3.

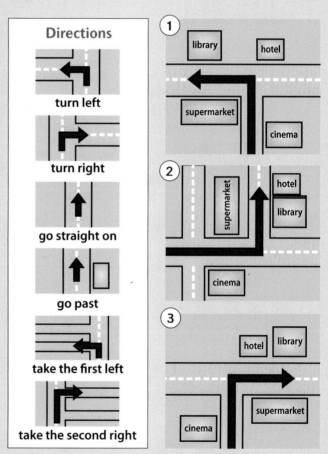

Directions
turn left
turn right
go straight on
go past
take the first left
take the second right

1 library / hotel / supermarket / cinema
2 supermarket / hotel / library / cinema
3 hotel / library / cinema / supermarket

b 🔊 **2.46** Match the two parts of the sentences. Then listen and check.

1 Excuse me, where's — A on.
2 Go straight — B the library?
3 Then turn right and — C repeat that?
4 The library is — D go down George Street.
5 Sorry, can you — E next to the hotel.

c Work with a partner.
Student A: Turn to page 121.
Student B: Turn to page 123.

Portfolio 9

Invitations

a Read the messages. Which one is not an invitation?

1

To Natalie

Dear Natalie,
Would you like to come to the cinema tomorrow evening? I'm going with Steve and Ben and then we're going to the café.
We're meeting outside the post office at 6pm. Can you come? Send me an email.

Love Caroline

friends online: 17

2

To Ethan

hello ethan what are you doing this weekend im going to the country with my brother would you like to come were going rock climbing and camping near, a river we're leaving at 8:00 in the morning on saturday speak to you soon, william

friends online: 6

3

hi trish i dont understand my science homework do you know the answers can you help me tomorrow we could meet at the library are you free

joel

b Look at messages 1–3. There are five sentences in message 1. How many sentences are there in:
- message 2? ......
- message 3? ......

c Correct the punctuation in messages 2 and 3. Use:

6 full stops (**.**) 4 apostrophes (**'**)
5 question marks (**?**) 19 **CAPITAL** letters

d Write a message (about 50 words) to a friend. Invite him/her to do something at the weekend. Before you write, think about:
- the activity you are doing
- the place where you are meeting
- the day and time when you are meeting

e Check your message. Is the punctuation correct?

PENGENNA PASTIES
simply the best

THE RECIPE
1 Order Your Pasties By Post
2 Products & Prices
3 Location Of Shops
4 About Pengenna
5 What's New?

WELCOME

Roll your mouse over the pastries to discover our delicious recipes

PENGENNA PASTIES

List Of Products & Prices

Traditional - Beef, Potato, Swede, Onion .... £3.00 each
Lamb - Lamb, Potato, Onion, Peas, Mint .... £3.00 each
Cheese & Onion - Mature Vegetarian Cheese, Potato, Onion .... £3.00 each
Vegetable - Potato, Swede, Onion, Peas, Carrots, Beans, Sweetcorn .... £2.85 each
Vegan - Potato, Swede, Onion, Peas, Carrots, Beans, Sweetcorn .... £2.85 each
.... £1.00 each

Porthminster Café
Porthminster Beach
St Ives
Cornwall

01736 795352

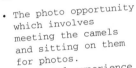

lusty Glaze
adventure

price list

Activity Type	Activity	RRP
Abseil & Climb	Cliff Abseil	£17.50
	Snakes & Ladders	£17.50
	Climbing Day (Off site – min 6 people)	£90
Surf School	Surf lesson (2.5 hours)	£35
	Body boarding lesson (2.5 hours)	£35
	Private Surf lesson (2.5 hours)	£65
	Surf & De-stress	£65
	Surf & Spa	£80
Beach Activities	Half hour beach volleyball	£6
	(Other beach activities available upon request)	

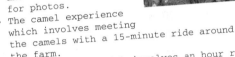

Roscuik Farm

Camel trekking

We offer three options to ride the camels:

- The photo opportunity which involves meeting the camels and sitting on them for photos.
- The camel experience which involves meeting the camels with a 15-minute ride around the farm.
- The camel trek which involves an hour ride on to the downs.

These cost £5, £18, and £50 per person respectively and we ask for payment on the day of the ride for convenience. Booking can be made either in person or by phone a couple of weeks before the date you choose to ride, so that we can set a date and a time. We accept card, cash or signed addressed cheques.

Mud
eden project

TATE
St IVES

International Modern and Contemporary

March–October
Daily 10.00–17.20, last admission 17.00

November–February
Tuesday–Saturday 10.00–16.20, last admission 16.00

Porthmeor Beach, St Ives, Cornwall. TR26 1TG
01736 796 226 • visiting.stives@tate.org.uk

ST. IVES
PORTHMEOR BEACH
HARBOUR
PORTHMINSTER BEACH

eden project

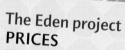

The Eden project PRICES

Adults	£15
Children (5 to 18 years old in full-time education)	£5
Seniors (over 60 years old)	£10
Under fives	FREE
Students (in full time education)	£7
Family (two adults and up to three children)	£36

EDEN SESSIONS PRESENTS...
LILY ALLEN
26TH JULY
STANDING - £27.50 + BF
ADMISSION FROM 9:00PM
NON-TRANSFERABLE, NON- REFUNDABLE
SEE WEBSITE FOR TERMS AND CONDITIONS, DIRECTIONS AND INFORMATION

1 Culture UK: Cornwall

a Look at the noticeboard about different places in Cornwall and answer the questions.

1 What's the name of the beach near the station in St Ives?
2 At the Eden Project, which is more expensive: a student or senior ticket?
3 What can you do at Lusty Glaze beach?
4 What's the name of St Ives' biggest art gallery?
5 What is the phone number of the Porthminster Café?
6 How much does it cost for a 15-minute camel ride at Roscuik Farm?
7 Which singer gave a concert in the Eden Sessions?
8 Is the Tate Gallery open every month of the year?

Cornwall

b Complete the puzzle and find the mystery word.

1 traditional food from Cornwall
2 an adjective to describe good food
3 the second month of the year
4 a place where you can have coffee
5 a food you often eat on the beach
6 people over 60 years old
7 a beach in Cornwall where you can play volleyball

c Work with a partner. Imagine you are in Cornwall for a weekend. What would you like to do?

2 Your project

What's on?

a Work in a group. Make a list of the most interesting places for tourists where you live.

b Plan a webpage. Think about:
- the best things to do / places to see
- opening times, ticket prices, etc.
- directions from the bus/train station to the centre of town
- pictures to put on your webpage

Porto Alegre

Casa de Cultura Mário Quintana Cultural Centre

Visits from Tuesday to Friday, from 9:00 to 20:00 and Saturdays and Sundays from 9:00 to 18:00

Beira-Rio Stadium

If you are a sports fan don't miss Beira-Rio Stadium. It is the home of the SC Internacional football team!

Mercado Público Central

With over 100 shops, there is a great variety of options for eating out: restaurants, fruit and fish shops, and a famous ice-cream parlour.

Open from Monday to Friday from 11:00 to 23:30, Saturdays from 11:00 to 20:00.

The Central Area Da Praia Street

Da Praia Street is the main street in the centre of the city. It has lots of shops, people and interesting things to see.

How to get to Porto Alegre

By Air:
There are many daily flights to and from Salgado Filho International Airport. There are bus services outside the airport terminal to take you into Porto Alegre city centre.

By Bus:
There are many bus routes from other cities in Brazil that stop in the main plaza in the centre of Porto Alegre. From there you can also find buses running across the city and to the suburbs.

10 Looking good

have to and *don't have to*
can and *could*: requests and permission
Vocabulary: Clothes; Accessories
Interaction 10: Buying clothes

1 Read and listen

a Look at the pictures. Read the text quickly and match the paragraphs with the pictures A–C.

The Interview: Toni, 16

Do you like Christ's Hospital? Yeah, it's a very friendly place. I love music and drama so it's great for me. I'm in the girls' choir and we made a CD last year.

Do you have to wear the uniform all the time? Well, most of the time.

Do you like the uniform? Yes. All the students voted to keep the uniform. We like it because it's different!

A SCHOOL WITH A GREAT TRADITION

1 ☐ He's wearing a long blue coat, short trousers and yellow socks. No, he isn't an actor in a historical film. He's a student wearing the uniform of Christ's Hospital, a private school in the south of England. Girls at the school also wear the traditional uniform, but they have to wear a skirt, not trousers. The blue and yellow uniform dates from 1552.

2 ☐ Today Christ's Hospital is an unusual private school because most students don't have to pay very much and for some students the education is free. Originally in London, the school is now no longer in the capital, it's in the country. With 5km² of grounds, the school is the largest in Britain. All students have to 'board' or live in the school. They also have to go to services in church on Sundays and Tuesdays.

3 ☐ Music and drama are very important at Christ's Hospital. The school has a theatre and performs a lot of plays and concerts. Most students play an instrument or sing. Every day, except Sunday, all the students walk behind the school band into the dining room for lunch. Twice a year the school band also walk in their uniforms through the centre of London.

b 🔊 2.47 Read the text again and listen. Are the sentences *right* (✓), *wrong* (✗) or *doesn't say* (−)?

1 Both girls and boys wear short trousers for school. ☐

2 The uniform today is the same as in 1552. ☐

3 Christ's Hospital is cheap for many students. ☐

4 There are more boys than girls at the school. ☐

5 Some students at Christ's Hospital live with their families. ☐

6 The school gives 12 concerts a year. ☐

2 Vocabulary

Clothes

a 🔊 **2.48** Match the words with the pictures. Then listen and check.

> **1** boots **2** coat **3** dress **4** jacket
> **5** jeans **6** jumper **7** shirt **8** shoes
> **9** shorts **10** skirt **11** socks **12** tights
> **13** trainers **14** trousers **15** T-shirt

Check it out!

Plurals for clothes
- Some clothes are always plural: *jeans*, *shorts*, *tights*, *sunglasses*.
- You can also say ***a pair of*** *jeans/shorts/tights*.

b When do you wear the clothes in Exercise 2a? Complete the table.

For school	At home	In summer	In winter	For sport	For a special occasion

c Do you know any more clothes? Write them down.

③ Grammar *have to* and *don't have to*

a Look at the examples and complete the table.

···▷ *Girls **have to** wear a skirt.*
*Most students **don't have to** pay very much.*

***Do** you **have to** wear the uniform all the time?*
*When **do** the students **have to** wear their uniform?*

Positive			**Negative**		
I/You/We/They	....	pay	I/You/We/They **don't**	....	pay
He/She/It	**has to**		He/She/It **doesn't**		

Yes/No questions			**Short answers**	
.... I/you/we/they	....	pay?	Yes, I/you/we/they **do**.	No, I/you/we/they **don't**.
Does he/she/it			Yes, he/she/it	No, he/she/it ....

Information questions	**Answers**
When **do** the students **have to** wear uniform?	Most of the time.

Circle the correct word(s) to complete the rules.

- We use *have to* for actions that are **necessary** / **not necessary**.
- We use *don't have to* for actions that are **necessary** / **not necessary**.

Grammar reference: Workbook page 98

b Circle the correct words.

1 Does he *has to / have to* walk the dog now?
2 I *have to / has to* see the doctor tomorrow.
3 Sara *have to / has to* wear a uniform.
4 You *don't have to / don't has to* shout. I can hear you!
5 She *don't have to / doesn't have to* go to work. Tomorrow's a holiday.

c Complete the sentences with the correct form of *have to* and a verb.

drive   get up   not go   learn   walk

1 We .... early tomorrow.
2 I .... German at school.
3 Jack .... to school on Saturdays.
4 In Britain you .... on the left.
5 Do we .... to the park?

d Put the words in the correct order.

1 have / Do / clean / you / your / to / room ?
   ----
2 you / to / have / Do / make / dinner ?
   ----
3 have / you / When / to / get up / on / do / Sundays ?
   ----
4 learn / you / to / Do / have / French ?
   ----

e Work with a partner. Ask and answer the questions in Exercise 3d.

④ Pronunciation DVD
/v/ and /f/

a 🔊 **2.49** We can pronounce have /hæv/ or /hæf/. Listen to the example.

Do you have much homework?
/v/
Yes. Do I have to do it?
/f/

b 🔊 **2.50** Listen and tick (✓) the correct column.

	/v/	/f/
1 Do you **have** much free time?	☐	☐
2 We **have** to wear a uniform.	☐	☐
3 We **have** Maths on Tuesdays.	☐	☐
4 Do you **have** to go to work now?	☐	☐
5 They always **have** a sandwich for lunch.	☐	☐
6 I don't **have** to get up early.	☐	☐

c 🔊 **2.51** Listen and check.

d 🔊 **2.52** Listen and repeat.

Victor and Fiona have to have five Fridays free.

⑤ Speak

a Look at the pictures. Where are the people?

b Make sentences about the pictures with *have to* and *don't have to*. Use the phrases.

> buy a ticket   use sun cream
> go with a friend   sleep in a tent
> be quiet   send invitations
> sit down   take a map
> cook on a fire   study   read books

c Work with a partner. Take it in turns to give rules and guess the place.

A: *You have to sit down.*
B: *A cinema?*
A: *No, you don't have to be quiet.*

⑥ Vocabulary

Accessories

a 🔊 **2.53** Match the words with the pictures. Then listen and check.

> **1** belt **2** bracelet **3** earrings
> **4** glasses **5** hat **6** necklace **7** ring
> **8** scarf **9** sunglasses **10** watch

b Do you know any more accessories? Write them down.

c Circle the word that's different.

1 hat / earrings / belt
2 watch / ring / bracelet
3 hat / necklace / scarf
4 glasses / earrings / sunglasses

d What accessories do you wear at school / at the weekends?

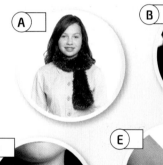  
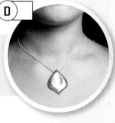  
  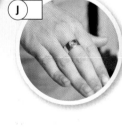

⑦ Listen

a 🔊 **2.54** Listen to the director and students of an English language summer school. Where is it?

b 🔊 **2.54** Listen again and choose the correct answer: A, B or C.

		A	**B**	**C**
1	In class students speak	Spanish.	English.	French.
2	In class students can't	eat and drink.	talk.	listen to music.
3	In class students can wear	jeans.	hats.	sunglasses.
4	Students have dinner at	6.30pm.	7pm.	7.30pm.
5	Students have to return to school before	10.00pm.	10.30pm.	11.00pm.
6	The school has got … computers.	three	four	five

(8) Grammar

can and *could*: requests and permission

Check it out!

can and **could**
- Don't use *to* with *can* or *could*.

a Look at the examples and complete the table.

> You **can** go out after dinner.
> You **can't** speak Spanish or Italian in class.

Can/Could I ask a question?
Yes, you **can**.   No, you **can't**.

Positive	Negative
I/You/He/She/It/We/They .... go out.	I/You/He/She/It/We/They .... go out.

Yes/No questions	Short answers
.... / .... I/you/he/she/it/we/they go out?	Yes, I/you/he/she/it/we/they .... No, I/you/he/she/it/we/they ....

Circle the correct words to complete the rules.

- We use *can* + verb to ask if it's **OK** / **not OK** to do something.
- *Could* is more **formal** / **informal** than *can*.

Grammar reference: Workbook page 96

b Put the words in the correct order. Then match the questions with the answers.

1 book / I / borrow / this / Can ?
   Can I borrow this book?

   A Yes, you can. Go and choose a DVD.

2 I / to / the / Can / cinema / go ?
   Can I go to the cinema?

   B Yes, she can but we haven't got the internet.

3 the / window / I / Could / close ?
   Could I close the window?

   C Sorry, I'm reading it at the moment.

4 Can / the / she / computer / use ?
   Can she use the computer?

   D Only if you finish your homework.

5 film / watch / we / Can / a ?
   Can we watch mov?

   E Why? Are you cold?

c Write questions and answers for these pictures. Use *can* or *could* and the word in brackets.

A: (go / party ?) *Can I go to the party?*
B: No, *you can't*

A: (have / sandwich ?) *Can I have a sandwich?*
B: Yes, *of course.*

A: (play / computer game ?) *Can I play your computer game?*
B: No, *you can't.*

A: (borrow / umbrella ?) *Can I borow Yes you ca*
B: Yes, *No, it's broken.*

Interaction 10

Buying clothes

a 🔊 2.55 Listen and tick (✓) what the customer buys.

1

2

3

b 🔊 2.55 Listen again and put the sentences in the correct order.

How much is it?	☐
Can I help you?	1
Here you are.	☐
What colours have you got?	☐
Great. I'll take it.	9
What size are you?	☐
I'd like to buy a T-shirt.	☐
Could I try it on?	☐
What colour do you want?	☐

c Work with a partner.

Student A and B: Turn to page 124.

Culture Vulture

Did you know that most secondary schools in the UK have school uniforms? Some students think they are a good idea and others hate them. Do you have to wear a uniform? Do you think they are a good idea? Why? / Why not?

Portfolio 10

A school uniform for teachers

a Read about a student's design for a school uniform for the teachers at her school. Make a list of the clothes and accessories they have to wear.

b Read the text again and put the paragraphs in the correct order.

1 What teachers wear now
2 New school uniform design
3 Extras for summer and winter
4 Conclusion

Cool clothes for teachers

☐ This is my design for a school uniform for my teachers. In the winter they have to wear blue jeans, a red and white T-shirt and a black jacket, but they don't have to wear the jacket in the classroom. They have to wear trainers but they can choose the colour.

☐ The teachers at my school always wear boring clothes. The men wear shirts and trousers and sometimes the women wear skirts. They always wear the same colours and they never wear jeans or T-shirts.

☐ I think the design is great. The clothes are more comfortable and fashionable. The teachers have to wear the uniform every day for school, but they can wear what they want at the weekend! What do you think?

☐ In summer the teachers have to wear black sunglasses. They can wear shorts when it's sunny. In winter they can wear a hat and scarf.

c Design a school uniform for the teachers or for the students at your school. Write a description of it. Use the text to help you. Before you write, think about:

- what they wear now
- the new design
- extras for summer and winter

Review ⑨ and ⑩

① Grammar

a Complete the sentences with the verbs in the present continuous.

1 We .... (go) to the library tomorrow to work on a school project.
2 They .... (have) a party on Saturday.
3 I .... (not watch) the match on TV tonight.
4 .... you .... (come) to our house?
5 She .... (not play) volleyball next Thursday. She's visiting her grandmother.
6 What .... he .... (do) today? ⬚ 6

b Circle the correct words.

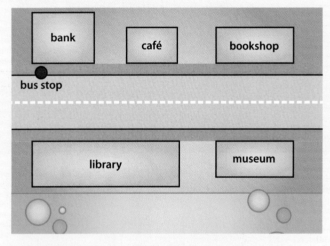

1 The museum is *opposite / in front of* the bookshop.
2 The bank is *next to / behind* the café.
3 The library is *between / next to* the museum.
4 The park is *between / behind* the library.
5 The café is *between / in front of* the bank and the bookshop.
6 The bus stop is *in front of / opposite* the bank. ⬚ 6

c Put the words in order.

1 I / Could / window / the / open ?
   ....

2 borrow / dictionary / Can / your / I ?
   ....

3 pass / me / Could / please / that / you / book ?
   ....

4 go / They / can / party / the / to
   ....

5 door / the / Could / you / close ?
   ....

6 help / me / please / Can / you ?
   ....

7 wear / trainers / can't / You / in / restaurant / that
   .... ⬚ 7

d Complete the sentences with the correct form of *have to* and the verbs in brackets.

1 I .... (go) to the dentist tomorrow.
2 My cousin .... (wear) a green uniform for school.
3 We .... (not do) our homework tonight. It's for next week.
4 .... you .... (go) to school on Saturdays?
5 They .... (run) 2km in PE.
6 I can't go out. I .... (help) my parents. ⬚ 6

e What does Tom say to Sara? Complete the conversation and write the letters in the boxes.

Sara: Tom, do you want to come to the cinema tonight?
1 Tom: ⬚
Sara: It's in the centre of town.
2 Tom: ⬚
Sara: No, that's another cinema. It's the big cinema next to the swimming pool.
3 Tom: ⬚
Sara: Yes, you can. Go to the bus stop and take the number two to the shopping centre, turn left and go straight on. It's on the right.
4 Tom: ⬚
Sara: Yes. We can meet five minutes before the film starts, at 6.25.
5 Tom: ⬚

A Can I get there by bus?
B Yes, that's a good idea. Where is it?
C 6.25. Great, see you then!
D Is it near the supermarket?
E Oh, I know where it is. Can I wait for you in front of the entrance? ⬚ 5

How are you doing?

How many points have you got? Put two crosses on the chart: one for grammar and one for vocabulary.

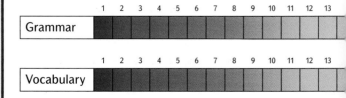

	1	2	3	4	5	6	7	8	9	10	11	12	13
Grammar													

	1	2	3	4	5	6	7	8	9	10	11	12	13
Vocabulary													

② Vocabulary

a Find 11 more words for buildings and places in the puzzle.

```
F P S D C I N E M A N I C Z K
X O U O T Q W K U O E G H J L
C S O Z C B N R S R S T Y U Q
V T I T X A G C E E J Q T Y S
B O D H B N F H U E R L U P N
N F S O L A O E M D A S W E S
M F A T H T L Y E I A J K V T
K I J E N I B L P G R H K C A
E C T L B X K Z G S C V C H T
W E H R J R K I E R R H H U I
B V A B A N K P U V O L U R O
Q R T P R W S H O P S U R C N
L I B R A R Y E L N T I N H U
A S U P E R M A R K E T O D I
F E R T S C H O O L P P O L S
```

`6`

b Match the shops (1–8) with the items (A–H).

1 a travel agent's   **A** some jeans
2 a pet shop   **B** some boots
3 a clothes shop   **C** a bed for a dog
4 a supermarket   **D** some aspirin
5 a shoe shop   **E** a book
6 a chemist's   **F** a newspaper
7 a newsagent's   **G** a train ticket
8 a bookshop   **H** some bread and fruit

`8`

c Put the letters in the correct order and make eight clothes words.

1 toac   ....
2 ockss   ....
3 esdrs   ....
4 nseaj   ....
5 irsht   ....
6 tirsk   ....
7 jetack   ....
8 ersoutrs   ....

`8`

GREEN: Great! Tell your teacher your score!
YELLOW: Not bad, but go to the website for extra practice.
RED: Talk to your teacher and look at Units 9 and 10 again. Go to the website for extra practice.

14	15	16	17	18	19	20	21	22	23	24	25	26	27	28	29	30

14	15	16	17	18	19	20	21	22	23	24	25	26	27	28	29	30

d Match the accessories in the box with the sentences.

> glasses   hat   earrings   ring   socks
> belt   scarf   sunglasses

1 You wear this round your neck when it's cold.
....

2 You wear this on your head.
....

3 You wear these on your feet.
....

4 You wear this with jeans or trousers.
....

5 You wear these to help you see.
....

6 You wear this on your finger.
....

7 You wear these on your ears.
....

8 You wear these when it's sunny.
....

`8`

Correct it!

Correct these typical learner errors from Units 9 and 10.

1 When are you comming to my house?
....

2 We are playing tennis the next week.
....

3 You can to get there by bus.
....

4 My bedroom is small and my bed is next the window.
....

5 I saw a very beautiful musium in the town centre.
....

6 Turn left and it's in front the school.
....

7 You haven't to wear a dress if you don't want to.
....

8 She have to come with me to the airport.
....

9 I coud join the club because it isn't far from my house.
....

10 Could I to have some information about your hotel?

11 Star quality

Present perfect: statements
Present perfect: questions
Vocabulary: Entertainment; Films
Interaction 11: Asking for and giving opinions

1 Vocabulary

Entertainment

a 🔊 **3.1** Match the words with the pictures. Then listen and check.

> **1** concert   **2** exhibition   **3** festival   **4** film
> **5** match   **6** musical   **7** play   **8** TV programme

b Complete the sentences with the words from Exercise 1a.

1 We're going to the cinema to see a ....

2 Did you see that .... about the rainforest on Channel 2 last night?

3 Who are Manchester United playing in the .... this afternoon?

4 Glastonbury is a fantastic .... with lots of music and events.

5 I'm acting in a .... at school with the drama club.

6 *Mamma Mia!* is my favourite .... I love the singing and dancing.

7 Do you want to go to the new .... at the National Gallery?

8 My favourite band is playing in a .... next month. I can't wait!

2 Speak

a Choose one of the things from Exercise 1a you did last month. Think about the answers to these questions.

- What did you do?
- Who did you do it with?
- When did you do it?
- Did you enjoy it?
- Where did you do it?

b Work with a partner. Describe what you did. Ask and answer questions.

A: *Last month I went to a concert with my cousin.*
B: *Who did you see?*
A: *We saw …*

Culture Vulture

Did you know that 50% of young people in Britain aged 15 to 24 go to the cinema once a month or more? How often do you and your friends go to the cinema?

3 Read and listen

a Read the text quickly and match the students with the jobs.

singer .... actor .... musician .... dancer ....

File   Edit   View   Bookmark   History   Tools   Help

Welcome to our website for the TV programme
STAR

Eighteen young dancers, actors, singers and musicians are living and working at the Star Academy for five weeks. They want to win a place at a top British school of dance, drama or music. But this competition is different because nobody knows how many prizes there are. The teachers have to decide how many students win.

Let's meet some of the students

Diana, 18, from Liverpool

Diana started dancing lessons when she was three. She left school at 16 because she wanted to dance. She's danced in seven shows and musicals in Liverpool. She loves Latin dances like Mambo and Samba and would love to dance in the Carnival in Brazil one day!

Lee, 16, from London

Lee didn't really like school and he wasn't a very good student. The only subject he enjoyed was drama. He says he feels like a different person when he is acting. He prefers theatre to cinema and he's seen lots of shows in London, but he hasn't acted in a London theatre. That's his dream.

Alex, 15, from York

Alex plays the piano and the guitar and he has written more than 20 songs. His parents are also musicians and his brother and sister play different instruments too. Alex's favourite instrument is the guitar and he plays it in his band. They have played at music festivals in York and Manchester and they want to be famous one day!

Jade, 16, from Bristol

Jade's family are Irish, but she lives in Bristol. She hasn't visited Ireland but she loves Irish music and she also sings in a jazz band. She hasn't won a competition before but she really wants to win this one. Everyone loves her voice because it's very beautiful.

Click here for more information about:
➡ the students
➡ the teachers
➡ the Star Academy
➡ the TV programme

Do you want to be in Star?
Click here for more information.

---

b 🔊 3.2 Read the text again and listen. Then write the name for each sentence: *D* (Diana), *L* (Lee), *A* (Alex) or *J* (Jade).

1 ....'s family are from Ireland.

2 .... He/She didn't enjoy studying.

3 .... wants to go to Latin America.

4 .... likes watching plays more than films.

5 ....'s family are very musical.

6 .... left school two years ago.

c What TV programmes like *Star* are there in your country? Do you like them? Why? / Why not?

4 Grammar Present perfect: statements

a Look at the examples and complete the table.

⤳ *He's seen lots of shows in London.*
They've played at different music festivals.

He hasn't acted in a London theatre.
I haven't won a competition before.

Positive: *have* + past participle			
I/You/We/They	**'ve**	**(have)**	**played**
He/she/It	....	**(has)**	

Negative: *have* + *not* + past participle			
I/You/We/They	....	**(have not)**	**played**
He/she/It	**hasn't**	**(has not)**	

Circle the correct words to complete the rules.

● We use the present perfect to talk about events or experiences in the **present** / **past**.
  We don't say exactly when they happened.
● The past participle form of a verb is normally **the same as** / **different from** the past simple.
● Irregular past participles **have** / **don't have** *-ed* endings.

Grammar reference: Workbook page 98

b 🔊 3.3 Complete the table. Use the irregular verb list on page 127 to help you. Then listen and check.

Verb	Past participle	Verb	Past participle	Verb	Past participle
....	done	....	heard	see	....
write	....	....	made	....	spoken
eat	....	meet	....	....	taken
have	....	....	read	win	....

c Complete the sentences with the verbs in the present perfect.

read   not see   not study   take   visit   win

1 The longest book I .... is *The Lord of the Rings*.
2 She .... the USA three times. Her aunt lives there.
3 I .... that film. Is it good?
4 I .... lots of photos with my camera.
5 They .... German before. This is their first year.
6 My team .... ten matches this year.

d Write six sentences about you: three true and three false.

⤳ *I haven't seen the film 'Hairspray'.*   *I've met Robbie Williams.*

● see (a film, sports team)
● hear (a band, singer)
● meet (a famous person)
● study (a language)
● play (a sport or game)
● eat (a food)

e Work with a partner. Read your partner's sentences.
Which are true and which are false?

5 Pronunciation 📀

/ɪ/ and /iː/

a 🔊 3.4 Listen to the /ɪ/ and /iː/ sounds in these words.

/ɪ/	ship	**it**
/iː/	sh**ee**p	**ea**t

b 🔊 3.5 Listen to the words. Circle the sound you hear.

live	/ɪ/	/iː/
leave	/ɪ/	/iː/
seen	/ɪ/	/iː/
sing	/ɪ/	/iː/
film	/ɪ/	/iː/
TV	/ɪ/	/iː/
written	/ɪ/	/iː/
eaten	/ɪ/	/iː/

c 🔊 3.6 Listen and check.

d 🔊 3.7 Listen and repeat.

He's been in a film and she's seen me sing on TV.

(6) Listen

a 🔊 3.8 Listen to the radio interview. What is Kerry Parker's job?

actor ☐ writer ☐ director ☐

b 🔊 3.8 Listen again and choose the correct answer: A, B or C.

1 Kerry has made …
  A one long film.
  B four short films.
  C five short films.

2 Kerry has won prizes for …
  A her short films.
  B her full-length film.
  C seeing 2,000 films.

3 Steven Spielberg was …
when he made his first film.
  A 16
  B 22
  C 23

4 Kerry hasn't met …
  A Natalie Portman.
  B Johnny Depp.
  C Scarlett Johansson.

5 At the moment Kerry
is making her film in …
  A Mexico.
  B France.
  C Monaco.

(7) Vocabulary Films

a 🔊 3.9 Match the words with the pictures. Then listen and check.

1 action film **2** animated film **3** comedy **4** drama **5** horror film **6** musical
7 romance **8** science-fiction (sci-fi) film **9** western

b 🔊 3.10 Listen to the music. Which films in Exercise 7a are they?

c What are your favourite films? What types of film are they?

⑧ Grammar

Present perfect: questions

a Look at the examples and complete the table.

⟶ *How many films* **have** *you* **made**?
   Have *you* **met** *any famous actors?*   *Yes, I* **have**.
   Have *you* **met** *her?*   *No, I* **haven't**.

Yes/No questions

| .... I/you/we/they | **met** her? |
| **Has** he/she/it | |

Short answers

Yes, I/you/we/they ....
No, I/you/we/they .... **(have not)**.
Yes, he/she/it **has**.
No, he/she/it **hasn't (has not)**.

Information questions   **Answers**
How many **films** have you **seen**? │ About 2,000.

Circle the correct word to complete the rule.

● We ask present perfect questions when we
  are interested in **when** / **if** somebody has done
  something.

Grammar reference: Workbook page 98

b 🔊 **3.11** Put the words in the correct order.
Then listen and check.

1 English / in / read / a / Have / you / book ?
  ....

2 Have / the / theatre / seen / the / play / at / you ?
  ....

3 she / a / Has / famous / person / met ?
  ....

4 heard / Has / their / he / latest / album ?
  ....

c 🔊 **3.12** Listen and write the short answers to
the questions.

d Work with a partner. Ask and answer the questions.
Use the present perfect.

1 watch / a basketball match? ....
2 win / a competition? ....
3 see / a play? ....
4 see / a musical? ....
5 eat / Mexican food? ....
6 meet / a famous person? ....

A: *Have you met a famous person?*
B: *Yes, I have. I've met …*

Interaction 11 ⬛DVD

Asking for and giving opinions

a 🔊 **3.13** Circle the correct opinions.

1 wonderful   OK   terrible
2 great   rubbish   OK

b 🔊 **3.13** Listen again and complete
the questions.

1 Have .... any films this
  month?
2 Was it .... ?
3 What .... it about?
4 .... did you go with?
5 .... don't you go and see it?
6 What do you .... of it?
7 What type of .... do you like ?

c Work with a partner.

Student A: Turn to page 121.
Student B: Turn to page 123.

Portfolio 11 A film review

a Read the film review. Did Charlie like the film?

Star review of the month

Have you **red** Alice in Wonderland, by Lewis Carroll? I did and I really liked it. It's an adventure story full of magic and danger. Yesterday I saw Tim Burton's version of the film at the cinema.

This story is about Alice, who is now a teenager. A man wants to marry her, but she runs away and falls down a rabbit hole. She travels **too** Wonderland, which she has visited before as a child, and **meats** lots of amazing characters on her adventures.

Their is a lot of good animation in the film. The Red Queen, played by Helena Bonham Carter, is very scary, and Johnny Depp is brilliant as the Mad Hatter. He's acted in a lot of films before but this is my favourite one. Mia Wasikowska is good as Alice, this is her first big film and I think she's going to be a big star!

Overall, I think this is a good film **four** teenagers, but it's a bit long. You should **sea** it if you like fantasy and adventure, but don't go if you like romances …it's not a love story!

Charlie, Manchester, UK

Send us a review of:
* a book you've read
* a film you've seen
* a CD you've listened to
* a TV programme you've watched

b Read the text again. Correct the spelling of the six highlighted words in the text.

c Write a review (about 50 words) of a film. Before you write, think about:
- the title of the film
- the main actors
- what happens in the film
- your opinion of the film

Check it out!

Homophones
- Be careful! Homophones are words that sound the same but are spelled differently.
hear, here
two, too, to

BOLLYWOOD PAST AND PRESENT

WHAT IS BOLLYWOOD?

Bollywood is the name of the Indian film industry. It's nearly the same as Hollywood, but the 'B' comes from Bombay, the biggest city in India, now called Mumbai. Bollywood makes nearly 800 films a year; that's twice the number of films made in Hollywood. The films are made very quickly and some actors are in three or four films at the same time.

BOLLYWOOD: PAST

People made the first Bollywood film in 1899. At first the films were silent and then in the 1930s they made films with sound. The first colour films started in the 1950s, which showed the beauty of the Indian clothes and costumes often worn in Bollywood productions. Traditional Bollywood films included a lot of singing and dancing, but action films also became popular in the 1970s. At first people only watched the films in India, but since the year 2000 Bollywood films have become popular all over the world. Today Bollywood's biggest international audience is in Britain.

BOLLYWOOD: PRESENT

Mumbai is the home of the Indian film industry. Thousands of people work there as actors, cameramen, directors and extras. It is common now for directors to make Bollywood films in other countries, such as the USA, France and China as Indian audiences are very interested in other countries. However, international cinema has also come to Bollywood. In 2009 the British director Danny Boyle filmed *Slumdog Millionaire* in Mumbai. The film showed the lives of poor people in the city and won eight Academy awards.

THE FUTURE OF BOLLYWOOD

The future is good. Big American film companies like Warner Bros and Twentieth Century Fox are opening offices in India. This means more colour, more dancing and definitely more Bollywood.

Bollywood star Salman Khan and his waxwork model at Madame Tussauds museum in London. Which is the real Salman?

Preity, 15, wants to be a Bollywood star.

I've seen over 100 different Bollywood films and I love them all, especially the action and romantic films. I have dancing and singing lessons and I want to be like my favourite actress, Aishwarya Rai. She's amazing!

Bollywood stars Abhishek Bachchan and Aishwarya Rai got married in April 2007.

Name – Abhishek Bachchan
Born – 5 February 1976, India
Studied – Business
Languages – English, Hindi, French
Extra information – His parents were both actors.

Name – Aishwarya Rai
Born – 1 November 1973, India
Studied – Architecture
Languages – English, Hindi, Tulu, Kannada, Tamil, Urdu and Marathi
Extra information – She was Miss World in 1994.

INTERVIEW WITH BOLLYWOOD ACTOR ARJUN RAMPAL

Why is Bollywood popular in the UK?
There are lots of Indians who don't live in India. The films are an opportunity to share Indian culture outside India.

What do you like about Bollywood films?
I love the singing and dancing. I feel like a rock star.

What do you think about Hollywood?
I love Hollywood films but Hollywood and Bollywood are completely different.

1 Culture World: Bollywood

a Read the magazine page. Circle the things Bollywood is famous for.

> sport   singing   books   action   horror   dancing   romance   westerns   films

b Read the magazine page again and answer the questions.

1 How many films are made in Hollywood every year?
2 Are Bollywood films popular outside India?
3 What types of Bollywood film are popular?
4 Where do Bollywood directors make films?
5 How many different languages does Aishwarya Rai speak?
6 Why do you think Warner Bros and Twentieth Century Fox are opening offices in India?

c Find a word in the magazine page that means …

1 the companies involved in a type of business (paragraph 1)

   ....

2 special clothes that someone wears to make them look different (paragraph 2)

   ....

3 something that often happens (paragraph 3) ....

d Have you ever seen a Bollywood film? Did you enjoy it?

2 Your project

Cinema in my country

a Work in a group. Read about two actors from the UK. Then complete the table with information about actors and films from your country.

Actors from the UK		
Name	Emma Watson	Dev Patel
Date and place of birth	1990, Paris	1990, London
Title of film	Harry Potter films	Slumdog Millionaire
Year	2001–2009+	2009
Other actors	Daniel Radcliff, Rupert Grint	Freida Pinto
Actors from my country		
Name		
Date and place of birth		
Title of film		
Year		
Other actors		

b Make a poster with the information about films or actors from your country. Illustrate the poster with pictures.

12 Party time

going to
will: offers and spontaneous decisions
Vocabulary: Adjectives for feelings; Celebrations
Interaction 12: Making suggestions

1 Read and listen

a Read the text quickly. Where can you see the best fireworks?

b 🔊)) **3.14** Read the text again and listen. Are the sentences *right* (✓), *wrong* (✗) or *doesn't say* (–)?

1 The *Las Fallas* festival is at the beginning of March. ☐

2 People make the *fallas* with their friends. ☐

3 People make the *fallas* in one week. ☐

4 The festival takes place outside in the street. ☐

5 People spend a lot of money on fireworks, *fallas* and costumes. ☐

6 One problem with the festival is the noise from the fires. ☐

7 A lot of tourists go to the festival. ☐

c Are there any festivals in your town? Are they similar to *Las Fallas*? Why? / Why not?

QUESTION AND ANSWER:
Las Fallas Festival

WHAT IS IT? A week-long festival with processions, music and lots of fireworks.

WHERE IS IT? In Valencia, Spain.

WHAT ARE THE *FALLAS*? They're big sculptures made of wood and paper. People burn them at the end of the festival.

WHEN IS IT? The main festival is 15–19 March every year.

Jessie Osmond's travel diary, March 10

The best party in Spain!

I'm in Valencia this week. Everyone is working hard at the moment, but next week they are going to party all week long! I asked David and Marta, two teenagers from Valencia, about the preparations for the festival of *Las Fallas*.

David
The tradition of *Las Fallas* started when carpenters burned their old wood at the end of winter to celebrate spring. Now, big groups of neighbours usually make a *falla* together. They can take about a year to make! My brother's an artist and he designed our *falla*. He's worried because he hasn't finished and it has to be ready next week!

Marta
I live in a village near Valencia but I come and stay with my grandmother for *Las Fallas*. There's music, dancing and processions in the streets. It's a very noisy festival and it goes on all day and all night for a week. A lot of people wear beautiful, traditional costumes and they make paella in the street. It's always great fun. This year is going to be the best, I'm really excited!

David and Marta's advice for visitors:

- There are more than 700 *fallas*, so don't try and see them all.
- Go and see the *Nit del Foc* (the Night of Fire) for the best fireworks.
- The fires are brilliant, but very noisy, and some people are frightened of them.

② Vocabulary

Adjectives for feelings

a 🔊 **3.15** Match the words with the pictures. Listen and check.

> **1** bored **2** excited **3** frightened
> **4** interested **5** surprised **6** worried

b Do you know more adjectives for feelings? Write them down.

c 🔊 **3.16** Listen and ⟨circle⟩ the correct words.

1 frightened / excited
2 interested / bored
3 surprised / bored
4 interested / frightened
5 surprised / worried
6 excited / worried

d Work with a partner. Tell your partner what makes you feel excited, surprised, etc. Can your partner guess your feelings?

A: *A party.*
B: *Excited?*
A: *Yes, that's right.*

No School Today

③ Grammar

going to

a Look at the examples and complete the table.

> ⋯⟩ *I'm **going to** stay for the party.*
> *Marta **isn't going to** wear a traditional costume.*
> ***Are** you **going to** come to the festival?   Yes, I **am**.*

Positive				Negative			
I	.... **(am)**	**going to**	stay wear	I	.... **(am not)**	**going to**	stay wear
He/She/It	.... **(is)**			He/She/It	.... **(is not)**		
You/We/They	.... **(are)**			You/We/They	.... **(are not)**		

Yes/No questions			Short answers			
Am I	**going to**	come? help?	Yes, I		No, I'.......... **not**.	
Is he/she/it			Yes, he/she/it		No, he/she/it	
.... you/we/they			Yes, you/we/they		No, you/we/they	

⟨Circle⟩ the correct word to complete the rule.

● We use *going to* to talk about **the present / future plans and intentions**.

Grammar reference: Workbook page 100

b Complete the sentences. Use the positive or negative of *going to* and the verbs.

> buy   do   read   not go   tidy   visit   not watch

1 I .... my emails after dinner.
2 We .... the Taj Mahal on our trip to India.
3 They .... a film on TV with their friends.
4 What .... you .... next weekend?
5 He .... a car when he's 18.
6 I .... to the festival in June.
7 When .... she .... her room?

c Write sentences about these people's plans for the summer. Use *going to* and the verbs.

> do   go   have   play   speak   watch

Bonjour

Homework

4 Pronunciation DVD

going to /gənə/

a 3.17 Listen and circle the number of words you hear.

1 I'm going to play football.
   4   6   7
2 She's going to learn to drive.
   7   5   8
3 We're going to eat a pizza now.
   4   10   6
4 Are we going to go out tonight?
   6   7   11

b 3.17 Listen and repeat.

c 3.18 Listen and repeat.

> Gary's going to get a guitar and Gavin's going to go to Greece.

d Write sentences using *going to*. Read them to your partner. Use the pronunciation of *going to* in Exercise 4a.

5 Speak

a Work with a partner. Ask and answer different questions about your future plans and intentions.

A: *What are you going to do tonight?*
B: *I'm going to watch TV.*
A: *What are you going to watch?*
B: *I'm going to watch a film.*

What
Where
Who
When

go   see
watch   play
do   meet

tonight
tomorrow
in the summer
next week

b Tell the class about two of your partner's plans.

····> *Tomorrow, Sita isn't going to play basketball. She's going to see …*

6 Listen

a 🔊 3.19 Listen to Nihal talking about the Indian festival of *Holi*. When is it?

b 🔊 3.19 Listen again and complete the sentences. Choose the correct answer: A, B or C.

1 *Holi* is also called the festival of ....
   A light   **B** food   **C** colours
2 The festival celebrates the start of ....
   A summer   **B** spring   **C** winter
3 *Gulal* is special coloured ....
   A paint   **B** food   **C** water
4 People wear .... clothes.
   A new   **B** no   **C** old
5 People give .... as presents.
   A sweets   **B** fruit   **C** books

7 Grammar

will: offers and spontaneous decisions

a Look at the examples and complete the table.

⇢ *I'll **buy** you some paint and a water pistol.*
*OK, I **won't** wear my best T-shirt.*

Positive

I/You/He/She/It/We/They	.... **(will)**	buy

Negative

I/You/He/She/It/We/They	.... **(will not)**	buy

Circle the correct word to complete the rule.

● We use *will* + verb for offers and spontaneous decisions we make **when / before** we speak.

Grammar reference: Workbook page 100

Culture Vulture

Did you know that there are many unusual festivals in Britain? One of them is 'Cheese rolling'. People roll a big round cheese down a hill and run after it. The winner is the first person to catch it. Do you have any unusual festivals in your country?

b Complete the conversations. Use *will* and the verbs.

help   cook   open   watch

1 A: I can't do my homework.
   B: Don't worry. I .... you.
2 A: I'm hungry.
   B: Me too. I think I .... some pasta.
3 A: I'm too hot.
   B: I .... the window.
4 A: Are you OK?
   B: No, I'm tired. I don't think I .... the film.

c Complete the sentences. Use *will*.

1 I'm tired. I think ....
2 My bedroom is really messy. I think
   ....
3 Oh no! There isn't any juice in the fridge.
   I think ....
4 There's nothing good on TV tonight. I don't
   think ....
5 My sister doesn't understand her Maths
   homework. I think ....

Check it out!

will

● Don't use *to* with *will*.

(8) Vocabulary

Celebrations

a 🔊 **3.20** Match the words with the pictures. Then listen and check.

> **1** cake **2** candles **3** costumes **4** decorations
> **5** fireworks **6** guests **7** presents **8** procession

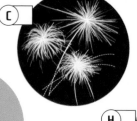

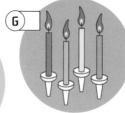

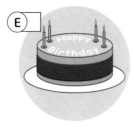
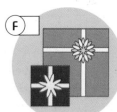

b Do you know any more celebration words? Write them down.

c Complete the texts with words from Exercise 8a.

> Last year we had a big party for my birthday and my grandma's birthday. My dad made us a chocolate ¹_____ . It was delicious. There were 80 ²_____ on the cake — sixteen for me and sixty-four for my grandma. Her birthday is the day after mine. The ³_____ were friends and family. I got lots of ⁴_____ but my grandma got more than me!

> This year we're organising a festival in my town. There are going to be lots of ⁵_____ in the streets — balloons and lights in the trees and shop windows. On Saturday there's going to be a ⁶_____ with people dancing in the street. They'll wear traditional ⁷_____ and at the end of the night there'll be lots of ⁸_____ . It's going to be very noisy!

d Work with a partner. Ask and answer the questions.

1 What happens at festivals in your country?
2 How does your family celebrate birthdays?
3 What other special occasions does your family celebrate? How?

Interaction 12 (DVD)

Making suggestions

a 🔊 **3.21** James and Sally are going to celebrate the end of the school year with a party. Listen and tick (✓) the things they're going to do.

> bring music
> buy drinks
> buy crisps
> buy ice cream
> make a cake
> make sandwiches
> phone friends
> send invitations
> buy pizza

b 🔊 **3.21** Listen again and match the two parts of the sentences.

1	How about	A	phone all our friends?
2	We'll need	B	lemonade and orange juice.
3	I'll buy those	C	an invitation by email.
4	Why don't you	D	food and drink?
5	Shall I	E	make the sandwiches?
6	Let's send	F	from the supermarket tomorrow.

c Work with a partner.

Student A: Turn to page 121.
Student B: Turn to page 123.

Portfolio 12

An email

a Read the email and (circle) the things that Marcus writes about.

> school   family   a celebration
> football   holidays   teachers

b Divide the main section of the email into four paragraphs:

1 exams
2 end of school year party
3 summer holiday plans
4 a friend's news

c Read the email again and find an example of:

- the past simple
- the present continuous
- *going to*
- a comparative form
- a superlative form
- the present perfect
- *will* for an offer

d Write an email (100–150 words) to a friend. Before you write, think about:

- your exams
- an end of school year celebration
- your plans for the summer holidays

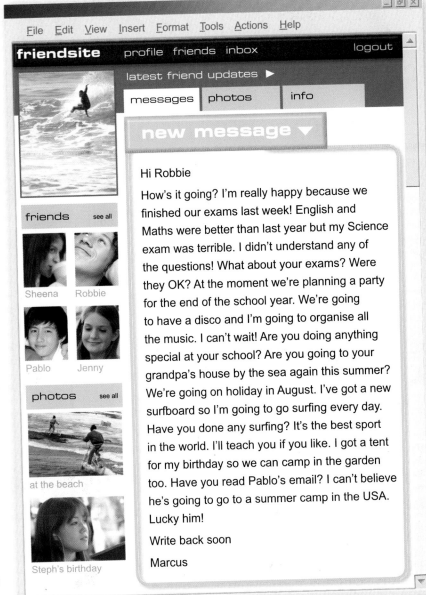

File   Edit   View   Insert   Format   Tools   Actions   Help

friendsite   profile   friends   inbox   logout

latest friend updates ►

messages   photos   info

new message ▼

Hi Robbie

How's it going? I'm really happy because we finished our exams last week! English and Maths were better than last year but my Science exam was terrible. I didn't understand any of the questions! What about your exams? Were they OK? At the moment we're planning a party for the end of the school year. We're going to have a disco and I'm going to organise all the music. I can't wait! Are you doing anything special at your school? Are you going to your grandpa's house by the sea again this summer? We're going on holiday in August. I've got a new surfboard so I'm going to go surfing every day. Have you done any surfing? It's the best sport in the world. I'll teach you if you like. I got a tent for my birthday so we can camp in the garden too. Have you read Pablo's email? I can't believe he's going to go to a summer camp in the USA. Lucky him!

Write back soon

Marcus

friends   see all

Sheena   Robbie

Pablo   Jenny

photos   see all

at the beach

Steph's birthday

Dancing in the Street

1 Song

a Look at the names of the cities and answer the questions.

> New York   Los Angeles   New Orleans   Chicago
> San Francisco   Philadelphia   Boston

1 Which country is each city in?
2 What do you know about them?
3 Do you know any other cities in this country?

b 3.22 Listen to the song and circle the cities in Exercise 1a that you hear.

c 3.23 Listen to the chorus and put the lines in the correct order.

Dancing in the street ☐

All we need is music, sweet music ☐

There'll be swinging, swaying and records playing ☐

There'll be music everywhere ☐

d Find pairs of words that rhyme.

> girl   meet   invitation
> nation   street   there
> wear   world

e 3.24 Listen to the next part of the song and complete the lines with the words in Exercise 1d.

Oh, it doesn't matter what you [1]............................ ,

Just as long as you are [2]............................ .

So come on, every guy grab a [3]............................ ,

Everywhere around the [4]............................ .

There'll be dancing

They're dancing in the street

This is an [5]............................ ,

Across the [6]............................ ,

A chance for folks to [7]............................ .

There'll be laughing, singing and music swinging

Dancing in the [8]............................ .

f Which two things does the songwriter think are important? Do you agree?

1 to have a good time with people everywhere ☐

2 people's clothes ☐

3 to travel around the USA ☐

4 music and dancing ☐

(2) Sound check

a 🔊 **3.25** Listen to the *-ing* sound at the end of the words in the song. How do you say it?

> *There'll be laugh**ing**, sing**ing** and music swing**ing**
> And danc**ing** in the street*

-ing ☐   -in ☐   -ng ☐

b Work with a partner. Complete a new verse for the song with eight different *-ing* words. Say the verse and pronounce the end of the words *-in*.

There'll be .... , ... , and people ....

and .... to the beat,

.... and .... and lots of ....

and .... in the street

(3) Musical notes

Dancing in the Street is a song from the 1960s by Martha and the Vandellas, an American group. At that time British music was also very popular. Lots of people all around the world loved British groups like The Beatles, The Rolling Stones and The Who.

Pop ☐

a 🔊 **3.26** Listen to some different types of music from the 1960s. Can you match the music with the pictures?

b Which type of music do you like best?

Mod ☐

Psychedelic ☐

Rock ☐

Review 11 and 12

1 Grammar

a Complete the sentences with the verbs in the present perfect.

1 He .... (see) a lot of horror films.
2 She .... (not play) volleyball before.
3 They .... (write) twenty songs.
4 I .... (not read) this book. Is it good?
5 She .... (listen) to this CD and she really likes it.
6 He .... (meet) lots of famous people.

6

b Complete the questions and short answers with the verbs in the present perfect.

> eat do take win finish

1 A: .... you .... Mexican food?
   B: Yes, I ....
2 A: .... they .... a competition?
   B: No, they ....
3 A: .... she .... lots of photos?
   B: No, she ....
4 A: .... we .... the milk?
   B: Yes, we ....
5 A: .... he .... his homework?
   B: No, he ....

5

c Match the phrases (1–7) with (A–G).

1 I'm hungry.
2 It's her birthday tomorrow.
3 That's a great film.
4 I'm tired.
5 They're on holiday next week.
6 I can't speak Turkish.
7 It's raining today.

A He isn't going to walk to school.
B I'm going to have a sandwich.
C They're going to travel around Italy.
D I'm going to go to bed.
E I'm going to learn it next year.
F She's going to have a party.
G We're going to see it at the cinema tonight.

7

d Circle the correct words.

1 A: My computer isn't working!
   B: It's OK, *I'll / I won't* help you.
2 It's sunny. I think *I'll / I won't* go for a walk.
3 Jake's busy. *I'll / I won't* phone him now.
4 A: It's a secret!
   B: It's OK! *I'll / I won't* tell Mum and Dad.
5 This is my school. *I'll / I won't* show you my classroom. Follow me!
6 It's Clara's party tonight but I don't think *I'll / I won't* go.

6

e Read Mark's email. Choose the correct answer: A, B or C.

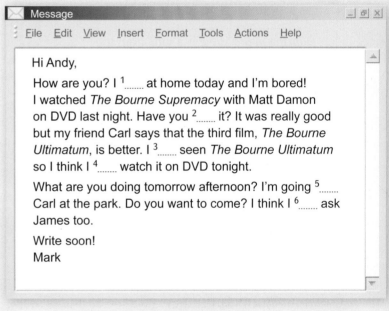

Message

File   Edit   View   Insert   Format   Tools   Actions   Help

Hi Andy,

How are you? I ^{1} ...... at home today and I'm bored! I watched *The Bourne Supremacy* with Matt Damon on DVD last night. Have you ^{2} ...... it? It was really good but my friend Carl says that the third film, *The Bourne Ultimatum*, is better. I ^{3} ...... seen *The Bourne Ultimatum* so I think I ^{4} ...... watch it on DVD tonight.

What are you doing tomorrow afternoon? I'm going ^{5} ...... Carl at the park. Do you want to come? I think I ^{6} ...... ask James too.

Write soon!
Mark

1	A 'll be	B 'm going	C 'm
2	A see	B seen	C seeing
3	A haven't	B 'm not	C not
4	A 'm going	B 'll	C won't
5	A meet	B to meet	C meeting
6	A 'll	B won't	C 'm going

6

How are you doing?

How many points have you got? Put two crosses on the chart: one for grammar and one for vocabulary.

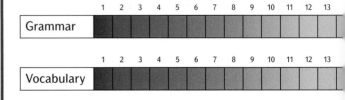

	1	2	3	4	5	6	7	8	9	10	11	12	13
Grammar													

	1	2	3	4	5	6	7	8	9	10	11	12	13
Vocabulary													

② Vocabulary

a Complete the crossword. Use the clues to help you.

Across

1 You see these at the cinema.
2 A play with lots of singing and dancing.
5 You go to this at a museum or a gallery.
6 You watch this on television.

Down

1 A place where lots of bands play – usually outside.
3 I like watching my favourite band play in these.
4 You go to the football ground to watch this.
7 Actors perform this in a theatre.

[8]

b Complete the sentences with the words.

action   animated   comedy   horror   musical
romance   science-fiction   western

1 I love _____ films. They're so exciting!
2 Have you seen this _____? It's really funny!
3 *Dracula* is the best _____ film I've seen.
4 My favourite _____ films have aliens.
5 There are always cowboys in _____s.
6 I watched this _____ last week. The singing and dancing are great.
7 *The Lion King* is an excellent _____ film. I love cartoons.
8 He falls in love with her. It's a beautiful _____ .

[8]

c Match the questions (1–6) with the answers (A–F).

1 What are you doing here?
2 What are you frightened of?
3 Why is he excited?
4 Is she interested in books?
5 Why are you worried?
6 Are they bored?

A I've got a Maths exam tomorrow! I don't really like maths.
B Spiders. I hate them.
C I'm visiting my cousin.
D Yes, she reads every day.
E Yes. The film isn't very interesting.
F Because he's going on holiday tomorrow.

[6]

d Put the letters in the correct order and make eight words.

1 ckea   _____
2 tsenpres   _____
3 refikswor   _____
4 cdlesan   _____
5 tucosmes   _____
6 ordecionsat _____
7 stsgue   _____
8 cesprosions _____

[8]

Correct it!

Correct these typical learner errors from Units 11 and 12.

1 Yesterday I have seen a bear in the mountains.
....

2 I have finish my homework.
....

3 I have wroten a postcard from Turkey.
....

4 Do you have heard this CD before?
....

5 She's going to visits a different city.
....

6 Next year I go to learn Chinese.
....

7 I am very interesting in this.
....

8 Don't worry. I will to help you.
....

9 Bye! I see you later.
....

10 I'm tired. I don't will go to the party.
....

GREEN: Great! Tell your teacher your score!
YELLOW: Not bad, but go to the website for extra practice.
RED: Talk to your teacher and look at Units 11 and 12 again. Go to the website for extra practice.

14	15	16	17	18	19	20	21	22	23	24	25	26	27	28	29	30

14	15	16	17	18	19	20	21	22	23	24	25	26	27	28	29	30

Skills 4 Real

UNITS 1-4

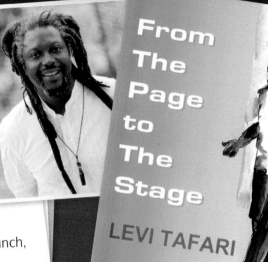

From
The
Page
to
The
Stage

LEVI TAFARI

Levi Tafari: Fact file

Date of birth: June 24th 1960
Place of birth: Liverpool
Poetry: *Duboetry* (1987), *Liverpool Experience* (1989),
Rhyme Don't Pay (1998), *From the Page to the Stage* (2006)
Films/TV: *The Road to Zion, Grange Hill, Blue Peter*
Music: work with Delado (Ghanaian drum and dance
ensemble), The Royal Liverpool Philharmonic Orchestra,
Ministry of Love (reggae fusion band), Urban Strawberry Lunch,
Dennis Rollins (jazz musician)

1 Speaking

Work with a partner.
Answer the questions.

1 Do you like poems?
2 Do you know the
  names of any famous
  poets?
3 Do you think it is
  difficult to write
  poems? Why? /
  Why not?

2 Reading

a  3.27 Listen to
Levi Tafari reading his
poem. What do you
think 'Reach for the
stars' means?

Reach for the Stars by Levi Tafari

BOOKS ARE COOL
BOOKS ARE FUN
BOOKS SHOULD BE READ
BY EVERYONE

BOOKS ARE COOL
BOOKS ARE FUN
BOOKS SHOULD BE READ
BY EVERYONE

Well, it's time to visit
your library
there you can borrow
BOOKS for free
BOOKS for the young and
BOOKS for the old
in BOOKSHOPS
BOOKS are bought and sold

BOOKS on poetry
BOOKS about sport
BOOKS that are long and
BOOKS that are short
BOOKS for girls yes, and
for boys
with sound effects
that make lots of noise

BOOKS about cars
BOOKS on trains
BOOKS about ships
BOOKS on planes
BOOKS on animals
BOOKS on religion
BOOKS that give you
INSPIRATION!

BOOKS with witches
casting spells
BOOKS that you can
scratch and smell
picture BOOKS
that have no words
BOOKS on insects
BOOKS on birds

Biographies
portraying people's lives
fictional BOOKS
on the edge of a knife
horror BOOKS
with a sting in the tale
BOOKS for people
who read in Braille

BOOKS on romance
BOOKS with passion
BOOKS on the famous
BOOKS on fashion
BOOKS on war and out of space
BOOKS about the people
of the human race

BOOKS that teach
you how to cook
you can even get
BOOKS about BOOKS
text BOOKS are used
in education
they are filled
with information

Now, if you really want
to succeed
choose the right BOOK
start to read
REACH FOR THE STARS
and you'll discover
now digest that BOOK
FROM COVER TO COVER

Because …
BOOKS ARE COOL
BOOKS ARE FUN
BOOKS SHOULD BE READ
BY EVERYONE

BOOKS ARE COOL
BOOKS ARE FUN
BOOKS SHOULD BE READ
BY EVERYONE

b Read the poem again. Match the words with the pictures.

1 library 2 ship 3 plane 4 train 5 witches
6 insects 7 birds 8 knife 9 Braille 10 cover

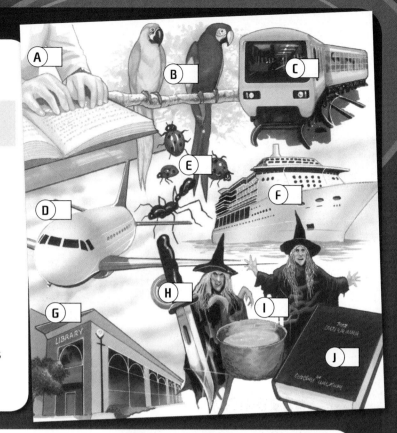

c <u>Underline</u> these words in the poem. Then read them aloud and match the pairs of words that rhyme.

old   sold

~~old~~ boys planes words birds
space noise race ~~sold~~ trains

d 🔊 3.28 Listen and check.

e Work with a partner. Read the first four verses of the poem aloud. Student A: Read verses 1 and 3. Student B: Read verses 2 and 4.

③ Listening

a 🔊 3.29 Listen to three people talking about reading. Make notes in the table.

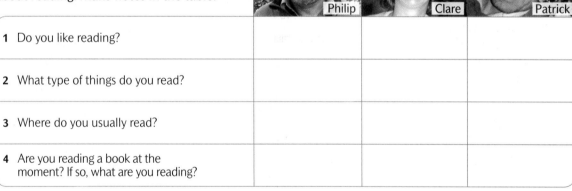

	Philip	Clare	Patrick
1 Do you like reading?			
2 What type of things do you read?			
3 Where do you usually read?			
4 Are you reading a book at the moment? If so, what are you reading?			

b 🔊 3.29 Listen again and check your answers.

c Work with a partner. Ask and answer the questions in Exercise 3a.

④ Writing

a Read the information about Levi Tafari's book, *From the Page to the Stage*.

> Levi Tafari's fourth collection of poems is called *From the Page to the Stage*. His poems are about many topics, including love, society and the environment. Levi is excellent at performing his work and these poems are perfect to read on the page or say aloud. I really like his poetry!

b Write a short paragraph about one of your favourite books. Include:
- the title
- the author
- the type of book
- what the book is about
- the main characters/subjects
- things you like about the book

1 Speaking

Work with a partner. Ask and answer the questions.

1 Do you like eating out?
2 Where did you go last time you went out for a meal? What did you eat?
3 Do you like fast food? Why?/Why not?

2 Reading

a Look at menus A–D from different cafés/restaurants. Where would you like to eat?

A Laurel Room Café

In the Laurel Room Café you will find an extensive menu to refresh you. Try our delicious selection of home-cooked foods.

Light Meals	Price
Soup of the Day	£2.20
served with Bread & Butter	£2.60
Panini	From £1.80
Mozzarella & Tomato; Tomato, Red Onion & Mozzarella; Chicken & Pesto Verdi; Mushroom, Leek & Tomato	
Omelettes	From £2.40
Choice of fillings, please ask Served with Mixed Leaf Garnish	
Jacket Potatoes	From £2.40
Choice of fillings, please ask Served with Mixed Leaf Garnish	

Light Snacks	Price
Sandwiches	From £1.99
Choice of fillings on fresh Brown or White Bread, please ask	
Toasties	From £2.15
Choice of fillings, please ask Served with Mixed Leaf Garnish	
Poached or Scrambled Eggs on Toast	£1.75
Beans on Toast	£1.40
Fruit Scone	70p
Toasted Teacake	90p

Opening hours:
10.00am–4.00pm Monday to Friday.

B Home café

Enjoy a drink and one of our delicious cakes in homely surroundings.

Beverages

Coffee	£1.50
Decaf coffee	£1.50
Espresso	£1.00
Tea per pot	£1.20
Speciality tea	£1.50
Hot chocolate	£2.00
Canned drinks	£1.20
Fruit juice	£1.00
Freshly squeezed orange juice	£1.50

Smoothies: £2.60
made with fresh fruit. Choose from two of the following: banana, strawberry, blueberry, kiwi, raspberry (in season)

Milkshakes: £2.00
banana, strawberry, chocolate, vanilla, toffee

Cakes

Farmhouse fruit cake	£1.80
Carrot cake	£1.80
Banana cake	£1.80
Double chocolate cake	£2.50
Sticky toffee pudding with custard	£2.50 / £2.80
Flapjack	£1.50
Brownie (house speciality!)	£1.50
Blueberry muffin	£1.80

Opening times
Easter – end of September   10.00am–4.00pm
Beginning of October to Easter   11.30am–3.30pm

C KING KEBAB

Eat in or takeaway
Opening hours:
12pm to 2am Tuesday–Saturday
12pm to 11pm Sunday–Monday

Kebabs	Small	Large	King
Doner Kebab Fresh seasoned lamb served with fresh salad	£3.90	£4.90	£5.90
Kofte Kebab Fresh minced lamb with parsley and herbs, barbecued on a flame grill	£4.30	£6.30	£8.30
Chicken Doner Kebab Seasoned grilled chicken served with fresh salad	£3.90	£5.60	£7.60
Special Chicken Kebab Chicken breast, barbecued with green pepper, onion & mushroom	£4.50	£6.90	£8.90

Curries			
Chicken curry:	£6.50	Lamb curry:	£6.50

Burgers			
Quarter-pounder:	£3.20	Fish burger:	£2.40
Half-pounder:	£4.00	Vegetarian burger:	£2.60
Chicken fillet burger:	£3.00	Hawaiian burger (with pineapple):	£3.40
Spicy chicken fillet burger:	£3.00	Garlic mushroom burger:	£3.70

All burgers with cheese: 30p extra

		Small	Large	King
Salad:	£1.20	Chips: £1.00	£1.80	£2.50

D

KNIGHT'S
FISH AND CHIP RESTAURANT

WE ALSO OFFER OTHER VARIETIES OF FISH – SURF OUR BOARD FOR CATCH OF THE DAY

Fillet of Cod and chips	5.95
Fillet of Haddock and chips	7.20
Fillet of Plaice and chips	6.95
Fishcake and chips	3.55
Cornish Pasty and chips	4.35
Vegetable Pasty and chips (V)	4.45
Plate of chips	2.70

I
J

PLEASE CHECK OUR DAILY SPECIALS BOARD FOR OTHER OPTIONS
(V) Suitable for vegetarians

Opening times		
	Mon	5–9.30pm
	Tues–Thurs	12–2.15pm and 5–9.30pm
	Fri–Sat	12–2.15pm and 5–10pm

b 🔊 3.30 Read the menus and match the words with pictures A–J. Then listen and check.

> 1 banana and raspberry smoothie
> 2 brownie 3 Cornish pasty 4 doner kebab
> 5 fillet of cod and chips 6 fruit scone
> 7 jacket potato 8 muffin 9 quarter-pounder
> 10 toastie

c Work with a partner. Which restaurant would you recommend for:

1 Someone who wants salad and chips with their meal?
2 Someone who likes fish but doesn't want to eat fish and chips?
3 Someone who wants a light lunch?
4 Someone who wants to drink traditional English tea?
5 Someone who wants to eat at 10 o'clock in the morning but doesn't like sweet things?

d Choose your favourite food from one of the menus.

3 Listening

a 🔊 3.31 Listen to three people talking about food. Make notes in the table.

Rosaline | Sam | Ellie

	Rosaline	Sam	Ellie
1 What's your favourite food?			
2 What do you eat for breakfast?			
3 Do you like going on picnics, and if so, what do you take?			
4 Is there any food that you really don't like?			

b 🔊 3.31 Listen again and check your answers.

c Work with a partner. Ask and answer the questions in Exercise 3a.

4 Writing

a You're going to plan a menu for your ideal café or restaurant. Include:

- the name of the restaurant or café
- the main dishes
- drinks available
- the price of the food
- the opening times
- any other information

b Swap your menu with a partner. Would you like to eat at his/her restaurant? Why?/Why not?

Skills 4 Real

UNITS 9–12

1 Speaking

Work with a partner. Answer the questions.

1 Do you like clothes? Do you think what you wear is important?
2 What fashion styles can you think of? Do you have a style?
3 Which celebrities do you think have a good sense of style?

2 Reading

a Look at the pictures of Lady Gaga. Do you like her style?

b Read the magazine interview. Who is Lady Gaga's favourite designer?

Lady Gaga: crazy or cool?

We thought you'd be a bit of a diva, but you seem quite down-to-earth ...
The truth is, I'm pretty extreme when it comes to rehearsals and getting lots of sleep. I can be really bossy. But I just want to do a good job.

OK, what about your outfits? Your style is mental!
Yeah, I don't think I'm weird. Where I come from, I'm cool. I'm different, my music is different. I don't think anyone was ready for it at first, but I made them ready for it.

We always see you walking around wearing amazing clothes. Even when it's freezing ...
For me it's not just stage clothes and then outside clothes. I've always been this way.

Have you always been into fashion?
I have, yeah.

'I'm different. My music is different'

You went to the same school as Paris Hilton. What do your teachers think of your *Just Dance* video?
I haven't asked them. I got a really solid education, in particular how to look at art, how to analyse art, how to make art. So if anything, my teachers are saying 'She did a good job using her abilities to create a new kind of pop music.'

Lady G's fashion faves

My top designer is ...
Chanel. Beautiful.

My style icon is ...
Morrissey.

I can't stop buying ...
Sunglasses. I have so many pairs – and never go anywhere without them.

Were you always talented?
I played piano from when I was four. It's the classical music that helped me to become a good songwriter.

Do you like being a star?
My album is about celebrity culture. I don't see myself as a celebrity. Hollywood, for me, is a very strange place – that's why I write about it.

c 🔊 **3.32** Match the words with the meanings. Then listen and check.

1	down-to-earth	**A**	clothes, shoes and accessories worn together
2	rehearsal	**B**	crazy
3	outfit	**C**	short, informal word for *favourite*
4	mental	**D**	practical and realistic
5	weird	**E**	practice to prepare for a show
6	fave	**F**	strange

d Read the interview again. Are the sentences about Lady Gaga *right* (✓), *wrong* (✗) or *doesn't say* (–)?

1 Her job is very important to her. ☐
2 Her music is similar to other pop stars. ☐
3 She is very interested in fashion. ☐
4 She was best friends with Paris Hilton at school. ☐
5 She didn't learn very much at school. ☐
6 She can play a musical instrument. ☐
7 She knows lots of people in Hollywood. ☐
8 She always has a pair of sunglasses with her. ☐

e Work with a partner. Ask and answer the questions.

1 Do you think Lady Gaga is crazy or cool?
2 Did you learn anything from the interview that surprised you?
3 Do you know any other celebrities who wear strange outfits? What do they wear? Do you like their style?

③ Listening

a 🔊 **3.33** Listen to three people talking about clothes and shopping. Make notes in the table.

	Sarah	Paul	Katy
1 What are your favourite clothes?			
2 What are your favourite accessories?			
3 Do you go shopping in town or do you shop on the internet?			
4 Have you bought any new clothes this month? If so, what did you buy?			

b 🔊 **3.33** Listen again and check your answers.

c Work with a partner. Ask and answer the questions in Exercise 3a.

④ Writing

a Think of a celebrity, past or present, whose clothes you like. Write a description of one of his/her outfits that you really like, but don't give the celebrity's name. Include:

● his/her clothes and accessories
● if the clothes and accessories are expensive or cheap
● if you think the clothes are crazy or cool

b Swap descriptions with a partner. Can he/she guess the celebrity?

Interaction: Student A

Interaction 1   page 10

c You are Balram Chandan. Read about you. Then take it in turns to ask questions and complete the table for your partner. Use the Interaction language on the front and back cover to help you.

Questions	You	Your partner
name	Balram Chandan	
age	14	
lives in	England	
lives with	mother and father	
pets	–	
favourite thing	bike	
languages	English and Hindi	

d Now compare your table with your partner's table.

Interaction 2   page 18

c Take it in turns to ask questions and complete the table for your partner. Use the Interaction language to help you.

How often do you ... ?	often	sometimes	hardly ever	never
get up late				
have breakfast with your family				
listen to music				
watch TV				
go to the cinema				
play computer games				
go shopping				

d Tell the class two things about your partner.

Interaction 3   page 28

c Find eight differences between what is happening in your picture and your partner's picture. Take it in turns to ask questions. Use the Interaction language to help you.

Interaction 4   page 36

c Look at the information about you. Talk to your partner and find a sport that you both want to do. Use the Interaction language to help you.

What sport do you want to do?		
	You	Your partner
like	team sports	
don't like	athletics, football	
good at	bouncing a ball	
bad at	tennis, rugby	

Interaction 5   page 47

c Take it in turns to describe two famous people to your partner. Can he/she guess who the famous people are? Use the Interaction language to help you.

1
(Gisele Bündchen)
Born: Rio Grande do Sul, Brazil, 1980
Job: model
Hair: long, blonde
Eyes: blue
Clue: She's got four sisters.

2
(Daniel Radcliffe)
Born: London, UK, 1989
Job: actor
Hair: short, brown
Eyes: blue
Clue: He was Harry Potter.

Interaction 6   page 54

c Read the text. Then take it in turns to ask questions and complete it. Use the Interaction language to help you. Your partner starts.

Tarik and his sister Safiye went on holiday to Turkey in 2010. They walked in a ² .... (*where / walk?*) and went to a mountain called Palmut. The weather was hot and sunny. They took lots of ⁴ .... (*what / take?*) and they bought some souvenirs. They went to Ciftik beach and saw some ⁶ .... (*what / see?*). Safiye saw her friend. She was on holiday too. Then they swam in a ⁸ .... (*where / swim?*). They had a great time.

d Now compare your answers.

Interaction 8   page 73

c Describe this room to your partner. Use the Interaction language to help you.

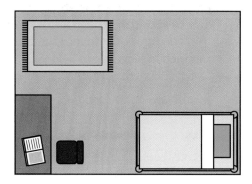

d Now listen to your partner's description. Draw the room he/she describes.

e Compare your pictures.

Interaction 9   page 82

c Ask your partner for directions to these places and write them on the map. Use the Interaction language to help you.
- the post office
- the swimming pool
- the Bluebell Café

d Now answer your partner's questions and give directions.

Interaction 11   page 100

c Take it in turns to ask questions. Complete the table about your partner. Use the Interaction language to help you.

Have you ...	✓/✗	Extra information
1 seen (a TV programme)?		
2 catcn (a type of food)?		
3 listened to (a CD / a song)?		
4 played (an instrument / a computer game)?		

Interaction 12   page 108

c Plan a party with your partner. Who is going to do these jobs? Use the Interaction language to help you.

Bring music   Buy drinks
Buy food   Buy ice cream
Make a cake   Make sandwiches
Phone friends   Send invitations

Your information
- You've got lots of CDs.
- You can go to the supermarket.
- You've got some bread and chicken.
- You can cook.
- You haven't got a computer.

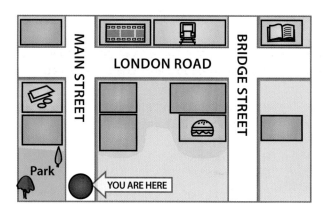

Interaction: Student B

Interaction 1 — page 10

c You are Giulietta Borsi. Read about you. Then take it in turns to ask questions. Complete the table for your partner. Use the Interaction language on the front and back cover to help you.

Questions	You	Your partner
name	Giulietta Borsi	
age	16	
lives in	Switzerland	
lives with	mother and sister	
pets	a cat	
favourite thing	mobile	
languages	Italian and English	

d Now compare your table with your partner's table.

Interaction 2 — page 18

c Take it in turns to ask questions and complete the table for your partner. Use the Interaction language to help you.

How often do you ... ?	often	sometimes	hardly ever	never
get up early				
have lunch with your family				
read magazines				
go out with your friends				
do sport				
go online				
do your homework				

d Tell the class two things about your partner.

Interaction 3 — page 28

c Find eight differences between what is happening your picture and your partner's picture. Take it in turns to ask questions. Use the Interaction language to help you.

Interaction 4 — page 36

c Look at the information about you. Talk to your partner and find a sport that you both want to do. Use the Interaction language to help you.

What sport do you want to do?	You	Your partner
like	athletics, tennis	
don't like	judo	
good at	catching a ball	
bad at	football, volleyball	

Interaction 5 — page 47

c Take it in turns to describe two famous people to your partner. Can he/she guess who the famous people are? Use the Interaction language to help you.

①
(Cristiano Ronaldo)
Born: Madeira, Portugal, 1985
Job: sports person
Hair: brown
Eyes: brown
Clue: He is a very famous football player.

②
(Beyoncé)
Born: Texas, USA, 1981
Job: singer/dancer/actress
Hair: long, brown
Eyes: brown
Clue: She was in the group Destiny's Child.

Interaction 6 — page 54

c Read the text. Then take it in turns to ask questions and complete it. Use the Interaction language to help you. Your partner starts.

Tarik and his sister Safiye went on holiday to
^{1}.................... (where / go?) in 2010. They
walked in a forest and went to a mountain
called Palmut. The weather was ^{3}....................
(what / weather / like?). They took lots of
photos and they bought some ^{5}....................
(what / buy?). They went to Ciftik beach and
saw some dolphins. Safiye saw ^{7}....................
(who / see?). She was on holiday too. Then
they swam in a lake. They had a great time.

d Now compare your answers.

Interaction 8 — page 73

c Listen to your partner. Draw the room he/she describes. Use the Interaction language to help you.

d Now describe this room to your partner.

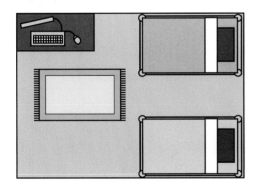

e Compare your pictures.

Interaction 9 — page 82

c Answer your partner's questions and give directions.

d Now ask your partner for directions to these places and write them on the map. Use the Interaction language to help you.
- the library
- the Odeon Cinema
- the burger restaurant

Interaction 11 — page 100

c Take it in turns to ask questions. Complete the table about your partner. Use the Interaction language to help you.

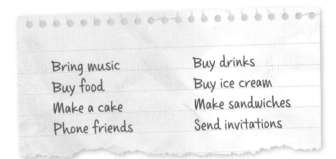

Have you ...	✓/✗	Extra information
1 visited (a place / country)?		
2 read (a book)?		
3 been to (a play / a concert)?		
4 watched (a film)?		

Interaction 12 — page 108

c Plan a party with your partner. Who is going to do these jobs? Use the Interaction language to help you.

Bring music   Buy drinks
Buy food   Buy ice cream
Make a cake   Make sandwiches
Phone friends   Send invitations

Your information
- You've got some lemonade and fruit juice.
- You don't really like cooking.
- You don't have a mobile phone.
- You've got a computer.
- You like art.

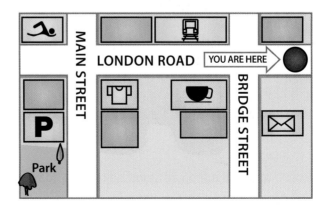

Interaction: Students A and B

Interaction 7   page 64

c   Student A: You are the waiter/waitress. Decide on three things on the menu that you haven't got. Ask the customer what he/she would like. Tell him/her the total.

Student B: You are the customer. Look at the menu and ask for food and drink.

Use the Interaction language to help you.

MENU

FOOD

Burgers (chicken burger, cheeseburger)	£1.60, £1.80
Pizzas (ham, cheese and tomato)	£1.65
Chips (small, medium, large)	40p, 55p, 70p
Sandwiches (cheese, ham, tuna)	£1.70
Soup (carrot, chicken)	£1.50
Ice cream (strawberry, vanilla, chocolate)	£1.20

DRINKS

Lemonade	80p
Juice (orange, apple, tomato)	95p
Tea, coffee	£1.00

d   Now change roles.

Student A: You are the customer. Look at the menu and ask for food and drink.

Student B: You are the waiter/waitress. Decide on three things on the menu that you haven't got. Ask the customer what he/she would like. Tell him/her the total.

Interaction 10   page 91

c   Look at the picture and imagine you are in this shop.

Student A: You are the customer. What do you want to buy? Ask the shop assistant for help.

Student B: You are the shop assistant. Help the customer.

Use the Interaction language to help you.

d   Now change roles.

Student A: You are the shop assistant. Help the customer.

Student B: You are the customer. What do you want to buy? Ask the shop assistant for help.

Wordlist

(adj) = adjective   (n) = noun   (npl) = plural noun   (v) = verb

Unit 1

Family

mother (n) /'mʌðə/
father (n) /'faːðə/
wife (n) /waɪf/
husband (n) /'hʌzbənd/
grandmother (n) /'græn,mʌðə/
grandfather (n) /'græn,faːðə/
granddaughter (n) /'græn,dɔːtə/
grandson (n) /'grænsʌn/
sister (n) /'sɪstə/
brother (n) /'brʌðə/
daughter (n) /'dɔːtə/
son (n) /sʌn/
aunt (n) /aːnt/
uncle (n) /'ʌŋkl/
cousin (n) /'kʌzn/

Everyday things

bicycle (n) /'baɪsɪkl/
camera (n) /'kæmrə/
clock (n) /klɒk/
keys (npl) /kiːz/
lamp (n) /læmp/
mobile (n) /'məʊbaɪl/
newspaper (n) /'njuːzs,peɪpə/
photo (n) /'fəʊtəʊ/
television (n) /'telɪvɪʒn/
umbrella (n) /ʌm'brelə/

Unit 2

Daily activities

do homework /duː 'həʊmwɜːk/
get dressed /get drest/
get up /get ʌp/
go online /gəʊ ,ɒn'laɪn/
go out with friends /gəʊ aʊt wɪð
    frendz/
go to bed /gəʊ tuː bed/
go to school /gəʊ tuː skuːl/
have breakfast /hæv 'brekfəst/
have a shower /hæv ə 'ʃaʊə/
listen to music /'lɪsn tuː 'mjuːzɪk/

School subjects

Art (n) /aːt/
English (n) /'ɪŋglɪʃ/
French (n) /frenʃ/
Geography (n) /dʒi'ɒgrəfi/
History (n) /'hɪstri/
ICT (Information and Communication
    Technology) (n) /,aɪ siː 'tiː/
Maths (n) /mæθs/

Music (n) /'mjuːzɪk/
PE (Physical Education) (n) /,piː 'iː/
Science (n) /'saɪəns/

Unit 3

Holiday activities

buy souvenirs /baɪ ,suːvn'ɪəz/
go camping /gəʊ 'kæmpɪŋ/
go to a disco /gəʊ tuː ə 'dɪskəʊ/
have an ice cream /hæv æn ,aɪs
    'kriːm/
play games /pleɪ geɪmz/
ride a horse /raɪd ə hɔːs/
sunbathe (v) /'sʌnbeɪð/
surf (v) /sɜːf/
swim (v) /swɪm/
take photos /teɪk 'fəʊtəʊz/

Weather and temperature

cloudy (adj) /'klaʊdi/
foggy (adj) /'fɒgi/
rainy (adj) /'reɪni/
snowy (adj) /'snəʊi/
sunny (adj) /'sʌni/
windy (adj) /'wɪndi/
It's cold. /its kəʊld/
It's cool. /its kuːl/
It's freezing. /its 'friːzɪŋ/
It's hot. /its hɒt/
It's really hot. /its 'rɪəli hɒt/
It's warm. /its wɔːm/

Unit 4

Sports

athletics (n) /æθ'letɪks/
basketball (n) /'baːskɪtbɔːl/
cricket (n) /'krɪkɪt/
cycling (n) /'saɪklɪŋ/
football (n) /'fʊtbɔːl/
hockey (n) /'hɒki/
judo (n) /'dʒuːdəʊ/
rugby (n) /'rʌgbi/
skiing (n) /'skiːɪŋ/
swimming (n) /'swɪmɪŋ/
tennis (n) /'tenɪs/
volleyball (n) /'vɒlibɔːl/

Sports words

bounce the ball /baʊns ðə bɔːl/
catch the ball /kætʃ ðə bɔːl/
hit the ball /hɪt ðə bɔːl/
kick the ball /kɪk ðə bɔːl/
pick up the ball /pɪk ʌp ðə bɔːl/
throw the ball /θrəʊ ðə bɔːl/

Unit 5

Describing people

Hair colour

black (adj) /blæk/
blonde (adj) /blɒnd/
brown (adj) /braʊn/
grey (adj) /greɪ/
red (adj) /red/

Hairstyle

curly (adj) /'kɜːli/
long (adj) /lɒŋ/
short (adj) /ʃɔːt/
straight (adj) /streɪt/
wavy (adj) /'weɪvi/

Eye colour

blue (adj) /bluː/
brown (adj) /braʊn/
green (adj) /griːn/
grey (adj) /greɪ/

Body

short (adj) /ʃɔːt/
slim (adj) /slɪm/
tall (adj) /tɔːl/

Jobs

actor (n) /'æktə/
artist (n) /'aːtɪst/
business person (n) /'bɪznɪs 'pɜːsn/
dancer (n) /'daːntsə/
model (n) /'mɒdl/
musician (n) /mjuː'zɪʃn/
photographer (n) /fə'tɒgrəfə/
singer (n) /'sɪŋə/
sports person (n) /spɔːts 'pɜːsn/
writer (n) /'raɪtə/

Unit 6

The natural world

beach (n) /biːtʃ/
field (n) /fiːld/
forest (n) /'fɒrɪst/
hill (n) /hɪl/
island (n) /'aɪlənd/
lake (n) /leɪk/
mountain (n) /'maʊntɪn/
river (n) /'rɪvə/
sea (n) /siː/
village (n) /'vɪlɪdʒ/

Animals

bear (n) /beə/
bird (n) /bɜːd/
cow (n) /kaʊ/
dolphin (n) /'dɒlfɪn/
frog (n) /frɒg/
monkey (n) /'mʌŋki/
mouse (n) /maʊs/
penguin (n) /'peŋgwɪn/
spider (n) /'spaɪdə/
turtle (n) /'tɜːtl/

Unit 7

Food and drink

apple juice (n) /'æpl dʒuːs/
bananas (npl) /bə'nɑːnəz/
biscuits (npl) /'bɪskɪts/
carrots (npl) /'kærəts/
grapes (npl) /greɪps/
ham (n) /hæm/
lemonade (n) /ˌlemə'neɪd/
milk (n) /mɪlk/
onions (npl) /'ʌnjənz/
pasta (n) /'pæstə/
potatoes (npl) /pə'teɪtəʊz/
salad (n) /'sæləd/
steak (n) /steɪk/
strawberries (npl) /'strɔːbriːz/
tuna (n) /'tjuːnə/

Food collocations

carrot soup (n) /'kærət suːp/
cheese sandwich (n) /tʃiːz 'sænwɪdʒ/
chicken burger (n) /'tʃɪkɪn 'bɜːgə/
chocolate milkshake (n) /'tʃɒklət 'mɪlkʃeɪk/
orange juice (n) /'ɒrɪndʒ dʒuːs/
strawberry ice cream (n) /'strɔːbri ˌaɪs'kriːm/
tomato salad (n) /tə'mɑːtəʊ 'sæləd/
tuna sandwich (n) /'tjuːnə 'sænwɪdʒ/
vanilla ice cream (n) / və'nɪlə ˌaɪs'kriːm/
veggie burger (n) /'vedʒi 'bɜːgə/

Unit 8

Parts of a house

bathroom (n) /'bɑːθrʊm/
bedroom (n) /'bedrʊm/
dining room (n) /'daɪnɪŋ rʊm/
garden (n) /'gɑːdn/
hall (n) /hɔːl/
kitchen (n) /'kɪtʃɪn/
living room (n) /'lɪvɪŋ rʊm/
stairs (npl) /steəz/

Furniture and objects

bath (n) /bɑːθ/
bed (n) /bed/
cooker (n) /'kʊkə/
cupboard (n) /'kʌbəd/
desk (n) /desk/
fridge (n) /frɪdʒ/
rug (n) /rʌg/
shower (n) /'ʃaʊə/
sofa (n) /'səʊfə/
wardrobe (n) /'wɔːdrəʊb/

Unit 9

Buildings and places

bank (n) /bæŋk/
café (n) /'kæfeɪ/
car park (n) /kɑː pɑːk/
football ground (n) /'fʊtbɔːl graʊnd/
library (n) /'laɪbri/
museum (n) /mjuː'ziːəm/
post office (n) /pəʊst 'ɒfɪs/
shopping centre (n) /'ʃɒpɪŋ 'sentə/
station (n) /'steɪʃn/

Shops

bookshop (n) /'bʊkʃɒp/
chemist's (n) /'kemɪsts/
clothes shop (n) /kləʊðz ʃɒp/
newsagent's (n) /'njuːzˌeɪdʒnts/
pet shop (n) /pet ʃɒp/
shoe shop (n) /ʃuː ʃɒp/
supermarket (n) /'suːpəˌmɑːkɪt/
travel agent's (n) /'trævl ˌeɪdʒnts/

Unit 10

Clothes

boots (npl) /buːts/
coat (n) /kəʊt/
dress (n) /dres/
jacket (n) /'dʒækɪt/
jeans (npl) /dʒiːnz/
jumper (n) /'dʒʌmpə/
shirt (n) /ʃɜːt/
shoes (npl) /ʃuːz/
shorts (npl) /ʃɔːts/
skirt (n) /skɜːt/
socks (npl) /sɒks/
tights (npl) /taɪts/
trainers (npl) /'treɪnəz/
trousers (npl) /'traʊzəz/
T-shirt (n) /'tiː ʃɜːt/

Accessories

belt (n) /belt/
bracelet (n) /'breɪslət/
earrings (npl) /'ɪərɪŋz/
glasses (npl) /'glɑːsɪz/
hat (n) /hæt/
necklace (n) /'nekləs/
ring (n) /rɪŋ/
scarf (n) /skɑːf/
sunglasses (npl) /'sʌnˌglɑːsɪz/
watch (n) /wɒtʃ/

Unit 11

Entertainment

concert (n) /'kɒnsət/
exhibition (n) /ˌeksɪ'bɪʃn/
festival (n) /'festɪvl/
film (n) /fɪlm/
match (n) /mætʃ/
musical (n) /'mjuːzɪkl/
play (n) /pleɪ/
TV programme (n) /ˌtiː 'viː 'prəʊgræm/

Films

action film (n) /'ækʃn fɪlm/
animated film (n) /'ænɪmeɪtɪd fɪlm/
comedy (n) /'kɒmədi/
drama (n) /'drɑːmə/
horror film (n) /'hɒrə fɪlm/
musical (n) /'mjuːzɪkl/
romance (n) /rəʊ'mæns/
science-fiction film/(sci-fi) film (n) /ˌsaɪəns 'fɪkʃn fɪlm/ /saɪ faɪ fɪlm/
western (n) /'westən/

Unit 12

Adjectives for feelings

bored (adj) /bɔːd/
excited (adj) /ɪk'saɪtɪd/
frightened (adj) /'fraɪtnd/
interested (adj) /'ɪntrəstɪd/
surprised (adj) /sə'praɪzd/
worried (adj) /'wʌrid/

Celebrations

cake (n) /keɪk/
candles (npl) /'kændlz/
costumes (npl) /'kɒstjuːmz/
decorations (npl) /ˌdekə'reɪʃnz/
fireworks (npl) /'faɪəwɜːks/
guests (npl) /gests/
presents (npl) /'preznts/
procession (n) /prə'seʃn/

Irregular verbs

Verb	Past simple	Past participle	Verb	Past simple	Past participle
be	was/were	been	let	let	let
become	became	become	lose	lost	lost
begin	began	begun	make	made	made
blow	blew	blown	mean	meant	meant
break	broke	broken	meet	met	met
bring	brought	brought	pay	paid	paid
build	built	built	put	put	put
burn	burned/burnt	burned/burnt	read /riːd/	read /red/	read /red/
buy	bought	bought	ride	rode	ridden
can	could	been able	ring	rang	rung
catch	caught	caught	run	ran	run
choose	chose	chosen	say	said	said
come	came	come	see	saw	seen
cost	cost	cost	sell	sold	sold
cut	cut	cut	send	sent	sent
do	did	done	set	set	set
draw	drew	drawn	shoot	shot	shot
drink	drank	drunk	shut	shut	shut
drive	drove	driven	sing	sang	sung
eat	ate	eaten	sit	sat	sat
fall	fell	fallen	sleep	slept	slept
feel	felt	felt	speak	spoke	spoken
fight	fought	fought	spell	spelled/spelt	spelled/spelt
find	found	found	spend	spent	spent
fly	flew	flown	stand	stood	stood
forget	forgot	forgotten	steal	stole	stolen
get	got	got	swim	swam	swum
give	gave	given	swing	swung	swung
go	went	gone	take	took	taken
grow	grew	grown	teach	taught	taught
have	had	had	tell	told	told
hear	heard	heard	think	thought	thought
hit	hit	hit	throw	threw	thrown
hold	held	held	understand	understood	understood
hurt	hurt	hurt	wake	woke	woken
keep	kept	kept	wear	wore	worn
know	knew	known	win	won	won
learn	learned/learnt	learned/learnt	write	wrote	written
leave	left	left			

Phonemic symbols

Consonant sounds

/b/
bird

/tʃ/
cheese

/d/
door

/f/
fish

/g/
girl

/h/
heart

/dʒ/
jam

/k/
key

/l/
leaf

/m/
monkey

/n/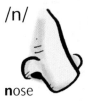
nose

/ŋ/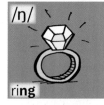
ring

/p/
pen

/r/
rain

/s/
sofa

/ʃ/
shoe

/ʒ/
television

/t/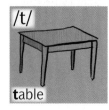
table

/ð/
feather

/θ/
think

/v/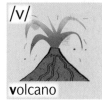
volcano

/w/
window

/j/
yoga

/z/
zoo

Vowel sounds

/æ/
apple

/e/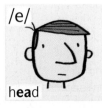
head

/ɪ/
insect

/ɒ/
hot

/ʌ/
umbrella

/ʊ/
book

/ɑː/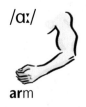
arm

/ɜː/
earth

/iː/
sheep

/ɔː/
ball

/uː/
moon

/eə/
chair

/ɪə/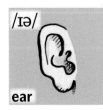
ear

/aɪ/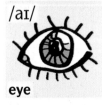
eye

/eɪ/
paper

/ɔɪ/
boy

/əʊ/
phone

/aʊ/
owl

/ə/
computer

Go to the Interactive website for more pronunciation practice!

http://interactive.cambridge.org